setting captives free

Purity Challenge
Training Youth in the Battle for Purity

Mike Cleveland
and
Nathan and Jena Wells

FOCUS
PUBLISHING

Purity Challenge
Training Youth in the Battle for Purity
by
Mike Cleveland
and Nathan and Jena Wells

Copyright ©2005 by Focus Publishing

Inquiries should be addressed to
Focus Publishing, Rights and Permissions
PO Box 665
Bemdij, MN 56619

ISBN: 1-885904-54-1

Cover Design by Michelle Hanevold

Printed in the United States of America

DEDICATIONS

We, Mike and Jody Cleveland, wish to dedicate this book,
with love, to our children Daniel, Joshua, Charity and Joy.
May you enjoy the eternal "pleasures at the right hand of God",
in the Person of Jesus Christ, rather than the "pleasures of sin",
which last only for a season.

We (Nathan and Jena) dedicate this book, with love,
to our boys, Austin and Samuel.
May you engage in the battle and see God.

ACKNOWLEDGMENTS

First, much gratitude goes to our Lord Jesus Christ for bringing us together. Thank you for showing us Yourself, and for satisfying the deepest desires of our hearts.

To our family: first our parents, Jon and Karen Sommer and Ron and Sandi Wells. Thanks for teaching and showing us the meaning of commitment. You have poured so much into us and have taught us much about God through your lives. We are so grateful! And to our brothers and sisters, thanks for your love, your accountability and for battling together with us!

To Mike and Jody Cleveland, thanks for giving us the opportunity to write and to partner with you in ministry. In Purity Challenge, you have opened up a door through which we are both humbled and excited to affect many for Christ. Thank you!

To the youth ministries at Shepherds' Grace Church and Ashland Grace Brethren Church, we thank you for helping us learn how to train you and others in this mighty battle for purity. Fight on young warriors!

To Lydia White and Mom Sommer, thanks for loving our family and babysitting so often so we could finish! Whew!

Anna Maupin, thanks for your fast friendship and your editing expertise! May you and your family continue to be blessed, and come visit us in Ohio!

And to the many students who have already completed this course online, thanks for your insights and granting us permission to use your testimonies to affect others.

Finally, to Jan Haley, thanks for your cheerleading, your graciousness throughout the process and your vision and heart to see many young lives affected with the powerful Word of God. You are a kindred spirit! Thank you!

With love,
Nathan and Jena

FOREWORD

By Dewey Bertolini

Dateline: The Garden of Eden

It didn't take long for the battle lines to be drawn. Soon after God created Adam and his lovely bride, Eve, God presented to the happy couple the Title Deed to a wonderland of unspeakable splendor, a priceless parcel of real estate where the Tigris and Euphrates rivers kiss each other, a lush land the beauty of which bedazzled their awestruck eyes. God placed only one prohibition on the newlyweds: They were not to eat of the fruit of one certain tree.

Everything was coming up roses for the first family, whose bright future brimmed with optimism. They loved each other. They loved and were loved by God. They had been commissioned by the Almighty to cultivate His beautiful Garden, to raise a family, and to commune with Him and with each other in intimacy forever. Life could not have been any better.

And then the Devil showed up. Satan promptly attempted to seduce Eve, and then Adam, into giving up everything. He made them an offer they could not refuse. This was his proposition:

> God knows that in the day you eat (the forbidden fruit) your eyes
> will be opened, and you will be like God, knowing good and evil
> (Genesis 3:5, NKJV explanation added).

The slithery serpent assured Eve that by eating the fruit that God had forbidden, she would actually take on a divine likeness in this tantalizing way: She would know good and evil in the same way God does. Eve, alas, succumbed to his irresistible offer.

Satan's promise begs the question, "In what way does God know good and evil?" The answer is only too clear: God knows good and evil by *defining* what is good and *defining* what is evil. God knows good and evil in this *determinative* sense: He, and He alone, writes the rules by which we live; He, and He alone, decrees what is right and what is wrong; He, and He alone, sits as the moral authority over His universe. He commands, and we obey.

The devil in effect offered Eve absolute moral freedom. He dangled before her wondering eyes the right to write the rules for her own life. He penned a "Declaration of Moral Independence" and coaxed Eve and her husband into signing it. And sign it, they did.

The battle is on. Satan's plan of attack is no different today. Paul warned his readers in Rome, "Therefore God also gave them up to uncleanness, in the lusts of their hearts, to dishonor their bodies among themselves, who exchanged the truth of God for the lie" (Romans 1:24,25). What lie? The offer, the promise, the guarantee, the fallen angel's absolute assurance that we can write the rules for our own lives; we can follow the lusts of our own hearts; we can eat the forbidden fruit of illicit sexual gratification whenever, wherever, however, and with whomever we want. The only detail the devil left out of perverted proposition was the price tag: the devastation that inevitably and invariably results from one's immoral choices.

Young people are today his target-of-choice. Satan sings to them the very same song.

But God sings a different song. His chorus goes like this: "But where sin abounded, grace abounded much more" (Romans 5:20). **Purity Challenge: Training Youth in the Battle for Purity** is a part of the fulfillment of this promise, a modern-day manifesto of God's grace in the lives of students who desperately want to know and follow His will vis-á-vis their sexuality. His voice echoes throughout every page of this fine book.

Mike Cleveland, and Nathan and Jena Wells are on a mission: to stand in God's stead, calling students on His behalf to a life of moral obedience. Their readers are young, impressionable souls whose entire lives lay before them, filled to overflowing with unlimited promise and potential. Their adversary is the destroyer (Revelation 9:11) whose perverted plan is to derail these precious young people with his lies, leaving devastation and destruction in his wake. Their Helper is the Holy Spirit, ever ready to convict students of sexual sin, to empower teenagers to make righteous choices, and to warn young people of the consequences of rebellious choices (John 16:8).

As young people read this book, a "great cloud of witnesses" will gather to cheer them on to "lay aside every...sin which so easily ensnares" them (Hebrews 12:1). Behind the scenes, the forces of good and evil will collide in a titanic battle to win the minds and hearts of these dear students. Mike, Nathan, and Jena have willingly jumped into fray to tackle head-on this serious subject. They have done their jobs well. The scores of students who, as the result of reading **Purity Challenge**, determine to make moral choices, and thereby to enjoy God's blessing, will be the lasting fruit of their faithful labor.

INTRODUCTION

"Blessed are the pure in heart, for they will see God" (Matthew 5:8). These powerful words from Jesus are the goal of Purity Challenge. As you work through this book you will be challenged directly in the area of sexual purity; but, don't lose sight of this great promise found in Matthew 5:8. *Seeing God* is the point! If all we do is talk about God in our lives, families and churches and never get to the wonderful place of *seeing Him* we are not experiencing what Jesus wants for us, and we'll never be fulfilled in the deepest places of our hearts and souls. As you engage this adventure of Purity Challenge, remember that you are in training for the Battle for Purity. Understand that our great desire for you is to *see God*, by faith while you walk the planet earth and then one day when you see Jesus face to face. The prerequisite to *seeing God* is being *pure in heart* and the only way for that to happen is to become increasingly captivated by Jesus Christ above all other pleasures.

Each of the 30 daily lessons consists of Scriptures to Consider, a brief teaching, practical examples, testimonies from other youth, and questions to personalize the lesson. We encourage you to find an adult mentor who loves Jesus, to help guide you through this adventure, to hold you accountable to keep at it, and be someone with whom you can discuss personal matters. This course is designed to help train you in the pursuit of purity throughout your entire life, and the goal is to help you *see* and experience a blessed relationship with God!

With that being said, let's get on with the challenge!

PURITY CHALLENGE
List of Lessons and Descriptions

DAY 1
Purity...

Tom asked his mom and dad if he could go with some friends to see an R-rated movie showing at the local theater. "You know that we don't approve of R-rated movies," answered his dad. "There are things in them that neither adults nor teenagers need to be watching." Tom turned on his heels and stormed up the steps. Just before he turned the corner he piped, "You and Mom are so old-fashioned. That movie only has a few cuss words and one sex scene in it. It's not like it's a porno movie or anything."

Later in the evening when Tom had calmed down at bit, he was drawn downstairs by a wonderful smell coming from the kitchen. "Whatcha making, Mom?" he asked as he gave her a quick hug. "Well, I thought I would make you a treat tonight. A pan of brownies is almost ready to come out of the oven."

Just then the buzzer sounded and Tom's mouth began to water in anticipation of the savory treat. Mom cut into the moist, steaming brownies and put the largest one on a plate and handed it to Tom. Just as he was about to sink his teeth into the gooey delight, his mom said, "Oh, by the way, along with the flour, sugar, butter, cocoa, and baking soda, I added a teeny bit of Petey's dog doo-doo to the batter. But don't worry, it was only a small amount, you probably won't even notice it."

Were the brownies pure???   What lesson was Mom trying to teach Tom?

What is Purity?

For the next 30 days we will deal with various topics regarding purity. But first, we should all be clear about what "purity" means. So let's look at a definition of "pure".

Webster's Dictionary defines "pure" as: "free from anything that taints, impairs, etc.; unmixed, clear." By that definition, a gallon of water with only 1 teaspoon of something else mixed in would not be pure water. A bucket of white paint with only 1 drop of black in it is no longer a bucket of purely white paint. It must be completely free from anything else in order to be considered "pure". A little something added to the mix makes the whole mix impure. Purity means pure, not contaminated, mixed, or blended with anything else—not one small thing!

How else can we explain what purity is?

A long time ago, a man named Oswald Chambers described purity to college students like this: "... purity is something that has been tested and tried and has triumphed, something that has character at the back of it, that can overcome and has overcome."[1] What does he mean? For example, gold must be heated and melted in order to refine it from all impurities. It then becomes "pure" gold and is unmixed with any other substance. The gold has been tested and tried, and only the pure gold comes out in the end.

About purity, Elizabeth Elliot says, "Purity means freedom from contamination, from anything that would spoil the taste or the pleasure... It means cleanness, clearness—no additives, nothing artificial—in other words, "all natural" in the sense in which the Original Designer designed it to be."[2] All natural... living a life the way God created you is not weird, it should be natural! Unfortunately, sin has come into our world and contaminated that which was "all natural". So now we must pursue, even harder, the original way we were created to live - a pure life in relationship with God.

Purity must involve the whole person. You cannot be half-pure. Purity must be a complete lifestyle. Whether you are with your friends, family, or alone, a pure lifestyle is consistent no matter who else is around. Purity spans far beyond sex. It is being blameless in every area of your life. That's so difficult! But it's something to work toward and pray for help to become. For the Christian, it's our destiny in heaven! The moment we see Jesus Christ face to face we will be like him – totally pure and perfected.

Dear friends, now we are children of God, and what we will be has not yet been made known. But we know that when he [Jesus Christ] appears, we shall be like him, for we shall see him as he is. Everyone who has this hope in him purifies himself, just as he is pure (1 John 3:2-3, Explination added).

Question 1. Explain purity in your own words.

Question 2. Please write your thoughts about this statement: "You cannot be half-pure".

Understanding what purity is, naturally leads us to wonder <u>who</u> decided what purity is.

Who Defines Purity?

Is Noah Webster, Oswald Chambers or even Elisabeth Eliot the authority and standard for purity? They can help us understand it, but they are/were not perfectly pure people either. So who decided what purity is? Who can really show us what purity is? Well, the answer falls to one Man. His name is Jesus. Jesus Christ is our picture and author of purity. He is the only totally pure, totally perfect One. Read these words of truth about Jesus Christ:

He committed no sin, and no deceit was found in his mouth (1 Peter 2:22).

God made him who had no sin to be sin for us, so that in him we might become the righteousness of God (2 Corinthians 5:21).

Question 3. From the above verses, how much sin had Jesus committed?

Only someone totally pure can show us the difference between purity and impurity. Think about it. Imagine a really smelly, filthy, dirty person. Maybe they haven't taken a bath in a year. Imagine that "filthy" person trying to teach a dirty little child what "clean" means and trying to show them how to be "clean". It wouldn't work! A "dirty" person cannot give a true picture or standard of what "clean" is unless he is first clean himself. It's the same with purity. Only someone totally clean and pure can set the standard for purity and show us how to be clean and pure. Jesus Christ set the standard. He is the only Man to ever live a totally pure, totally perfect life. His is the life to which we can compare ours and get a good picture of where we fall in regard to purity. Jesus is the One true definition of purity.

Areas of Purity

As we said earlier, purity spans far beyond sex. A pure life involves every area. That is what we desire for you. We pray for you to learn to live a life that is pleasing to God in every area. Remember Webster's definition of purity: free from anything that taints, impairs; clear, unmixed. Using that definition, let's look at a few areas of life where purity can be evident.

- **Relational: (friends, parents/family, God)**
  Purity demonstrated in your relationships would mean freedom from lying, deception, selfishness, and disobedience. Purity is truthful, loving and selfless.
- **Academic:**
  Academic purity would involve no cheating!
- **Athletic:**
  Athletic purity involves no cheating, no dishonest gain, no selfishness, lying, or deception.
- **Entertainment:**
  Purity here consists of no activities or pictures (still or video) that tempt you or try to display impurity as something good.
- **Work:**
  Purity at work involves no gossip, laziness, deception, or disobedience.
- **Sexual:**
  This consists of no pre-marital sex, no impure thoughts, activities, or actions; not treating others (or allowing someone to treat you) selfishly; nothing inconsistent with God's design for you and your body.

Question 4. In which areas is it <u>easier</u> for you to maintain purity?

Question 3. In which areas is it most difficult to maintain purity? Why?

4

The following testimony is from Leah: When I began this course, I was not prepared for the life-changing effects that it would have upon me. Prior to doing the course I thought that I was pretty pure, I am a virgin and was planning on remaining that way until marriage, but in other areas of my life sexual impurity was rampant. Until I did this course, I did not understand that being sexually pure meant more than virginity, it is more than a physical state; it is also a spiritual, psychological and emotional state of being. This course taught me that being a virgin is not enough and that sexual purity is to be maintained throughout our lives, not something that is tossed aside after you are married. Until now I never thought of it like that.

After I started this course it became pretty apparent that the way that I was living my life was anything but sexually pure. I was hung-up on how far I could go while maintaining my virginity, and my mentor pointed out that this was not the right question to ask, that sexual purity was not a line but a way of living. I am now committed to that way of living. This course has equipped me with what I need to live a life of sexual purity, a life that is pleasing to God.

Some Important Things to Know as We Pursue Purity

Foundation 1. The truth is, there <u>is</u> a Moral Standard for a pure life. Society may lie and try to convince you that there is no standard, or that something can be right or wrong depending on each person and how you feel or would like to interpret it. But that is a lie. There is a moral standard and those guidelines can be found in the Bible. What the Bible contains is truth about God and His standards. We will base our standard for purity on the instructions and encouragement found in the Bible.

Foundation 2. There is Absolute Truth. Absolute Truth means it can never be proven wrong or found faulty. It is absolutely true, absolutely all the time. Absolute Truth never leaves room for an exception. You must know, there is Absolute Truth, and it is God and His Word, the Bible. God created us and everything in the world. God is perfect. So therefore, his Word will never be imperfect or untrue. He is Absolute Truth and His Word is absolutely true. You cannot ever prove Him wrong or find fault in Him. We may think sometimes that we know better or that God made a mistake, but given all the information God has, we would agree with Him every time. He is 100% true and His words found in the Bible are 100% true.

It is important to make sure you understand there is Absolute Truth and where it is found. It is our goal to direct you to the source of Truth – God revealed to us through Jesus Christ and His Word—so that you can discover a lifetime of Truth that applies to every day and every situation.

Scripture to Consider

Teach me your way, O LORD, and I will walk in your truth; give me an undivided heart, that I may fear your name. I will praise you, O Lord my God, with all my heart; I will glorify your name forever. For great is your love toward me; you have delivered me from the depths of the grave. (emphasis added) (Psalm 86:11-13)

Please take a minute and think about these next two questions. You will be asked them every day and you may get tired of answering them if they don't mean something to you. We want you to answer them truthfully. We're dealing with reality and truth throughout this whole course, so we want you to give us your answers based on truth, not just what you think should be the right answer. We desire for you to really dig and work through these important, but tough issues. To do that effectively, you must choose to be truthful and real.

Did you live sexually pure today?
     Yes   *No*

Are you committed to staying sexually pure?
     Yes   *No*

DAY 2
Challenge

Challenge: A Noun

A challenge: a test, trial, contest; involves endurance and difficulty

Erik Weihenmayer was born with a degenerative eye disorder that progressively unraveled his retinas. He lost his sight by age thirteen. Yet from early on he was determined to rise above this disability. In his book <u>Touch the Top of the World,</u> Erik tells of his struggles to push past the limits placed on him by his visual impairment and by a seeing world. Erik is a world-class athlete. He is an acrobatic skydiver, a long distance biker and marathon runner, a skier, mountaineer, ice climber and rock climber. Erik became the first blind man to reach the summit of Mt. McKinley, the first blind man to scale the infamous 3,300-foot rock wall of El Capitan and then Argentina's Aconcagua. He was married to his longtime sweetheart at 13,000 feet on Mt. Kilimanjaro. He is on course to reach all Seven Summits, the highest peak on each continent. Now, he lives in Colorado with his wife and daughter.[3]

Eric Weihenmayer understands the meaning of the word "challenge". To climb the highest mountains in the world is a challenge. To do them without sight is an amazing challenge! But the benefits that this man has gained in his life because he worked through and rose to various challenges are undeniable. However, those benefits would not be his, had he not worked hard to meet the many challenges he has had in his life. Here are some "musts" that are required of a challenge:

1. **A challenge must be something that is <u>not</u> naturally <u>easy</u> for you to achieve or accomplish**.
    Running a marathon, playing guitar, getting an A, asking a girl out, and keeping your room clean are not necessarily easy to do. But to challenge yourself, you engage in what's not so easy! Eating pizza, sleeping in late, hanging out with friends you like wouldn't be considered much of a challenge.

2. **A challenge must involve <u>obstacles</u>.**
    Think of the challenge of climbing a mountain. There are many obstacles that must be overcome in order for it to be a real accomplishment! If there were a paved highway up the side of the mountain, all obstacles would be gone and climbing it

would involve no skill, no work, no endurance. It would not be a challenge!

3. **A challenge must involve some kind of <u>risk</u>.**

   A challenge naturally involves an unknown or difficult outcome. Because of the unknown and the difficulties, there are also risks involved. There can be a risk of failure if you don't accomplish what you set out to do. There can be a risk involving personal changes that will need to be made. There can also be a risk of success if you succeed and all that will be required to maintain that success. Other risks may involve your relationships, or even your reputation.

4. **A challenge must have a <u>goal</u>.**

   The whole purpose of a challenge is to reach a desired goal. You wouldn't drag a sled to the top of a snowy hill if you could never experience sledding back down once you got up there. They don't hold marathons that have no marked course and no finish line. You don't start playing the guitar just so you can enjoy playing only the G-chord the rest of your life. There's a goal in mind! And there's always a best way to make it to that goal. Any challenge must have a goal to worth achieving!

As we learn about purity together, we will see that it will be a challenge not only to finish this course, but also to maintain a life of purity. That's okay! The difficulty, the obstacles, the risk and the goal of purity you seek, all prove that you are engaging in a true challenge! And in reality, it is God's grace that enables us to face the challenge of purity, and to overcome all obstacles in our way.

Yes, and all who desire to live godly in Christ Jesus will suffer persecution. (2 Timothy 3:12 NKJV).

Question 1. What is the challenge that awaits all who desire to live godly in Christ Jesus?

Question 2. What are your fears, questions or hesitations about rising to this challenge?

Challenge: A Verb

<u>To</u> challenge: to object to; to question; to accuse; to call to answer; to disagree and demonstrate your disagreement.

In a high school weekend soccer tournament, the last game of the day had just begun even though the sun was already setting. Rain earlier in the day had delayed all games by 2 hours. Even though this particular field had no lights, the whistle was blown to start the game with the hopes of finishing before darkness set in. The game was a close one, with a 1-1 score at half time. The two teams; the Lions and the Cobras had been rivals for years and the battle for the win was far from over. By the end of half-time, you could barely see across the field. Both coaches asked the referees to consider finishing the game in the morning. The referees declined, stating that there was still enough light to continue. By midway through the second half, it was so dark that the players had to really focus to tell their own players apart. All the shadows created by the encroaching darkness really did a number on depth perception and coordination.

By now both coaches were yelling for the game to be called for the day. The goalies at each end of the field had to guess what was going on, because they could not see the other end of the field. Just before the referees decided to postpone the game, one player for the Cobras got a break-away and quickly streaked down the side of the field, headed toward the goal. Not able to see what was happening, the Lion goalie began yelling for back-up. As his own players rushed around the lone Cobra forward, the soccer ball rolled just inches over the out-of-bounds line. However, before the ref could see it or anyone could say anything, the Cobra player took a big stride and nailed that ball right into the corner of the goal. The goalie didn't even see the ball.

Everyone on the Lion team was livid! Players were yelling that the ball was out of bounds, the ref was saying he didn't see it, and the coach was yelling that it was too dark and the game should have been called much sooner! The referees postponed the final 10 minutes of the game until 8:00 the next morning, but the Lions were not ready to settle for the loss. The coach of the Lions formally challenged the referees to take back the goal because the ball had been out of bounds and it was too dark to play well or referee fair. After many minutes of discussion, the referees decided to take back the Cobra goal, leaving the score 1-1, and re-play the entire second half of the game the next morning. Because the coach challenged a wrong call and a faulty standard for playing, he affected the outcome of the entire tournament the next day.

What are the set standards for purity in our society? Think of the "Reality TV" shows, movies, music. What standards are displayed? Do you agree with those standards that popular culture has set? Either you agree and remain quiet, or you disagree and must challenge those standards.

Question 3. If a teacher accuses you of cheating in her class, and you honestly know you did not cheat, what would you do?
- A.   agree with her, remain quiet, don't share the truth you know and take consequences
- B.   disagree with her, voice your challenge to the accusations, gently explain the truth and possibly avoid punishment

Question 4. Explain why you answered what you did in Question 3.

If you are included in something that is wrong, yet you never voice your thoughts or knowledge of truth to anyone, ultimately you are saying it's okay, and the consequences will be yours as well. The Evil One is the accuser. The Evil One sets morally deficient standards. We must challenge those standards with the Truth or we are saying they are okay and are in danger of the consequences ourselves! Instead, we must disagree and challenge society's standards of purity!

For it is God who works in you to will and to act according to his good purpose. Do everything without complaining or arguing, so that you may become blameless and pure, children of God without fault in a crooked and depraved generation, in which you shine like stars in the universe as you hold out the word of life (Philippians 2:13-16a).

Question 5. How are we to "challenge" the crooked and depraved generation in which we live?

Question 6. What does Philippians 2:13-16a tell us to hold out? Why?

Although they [the wicked] know God's righteous decree that those who do such things [sin] deserve death, they not only continue to do these very things [sin] but also approve of those who practice them. (Romans 1:32, explanation added).

Question 7. Who approves of those who practice sin and evil?

Question 8. Do your words and actions challenge the evil in your generation, or by not challenging them are you guilty of approving them? Please spend a few minutes talking to God about your answer here.

Testimony from Matt: Purity is so counter-cultural. People think I'm retarded sometimes, but I just have to laugh and keep my path and know that as long as I'm following Jesus, nothing else matters. I know purity includes sexual aspects but it also includes many others and I'll be working on those until the day I die.

Testimony from Laura: I began hanging out with a group of friends who weren't a good influence on me at all. At first I thought that I could influence them for the better, but it ended up being the other way around and I did so many things that I am not very proud of. Two years later, I began dating a non-Christian. I prayed that instead of going downhill I could be a good influence on him. I decided it was very important to share what I believed with my boyfriend. I became a stronger Christian by trying to be a good example to him of what a Christian should be. Six months later he became a Christian. Since then, things have not always been perfect, but they have been really great.

Scripture to Consider

So I tell you this, and insist on it in the Lord, that you must no longer live as the Gentiles do, in the futility of their thinking. They are darkened in their understanding and separated from the life of God because of the ignorance that is in them due to the hardening of their hearts. Having lost all sensitivity, they have given themselves over to sensuality so as to indulge in every kind of impurity, with a continual lust for more. You, however did not come to know Christ that way. Surely you heard of him and were taught in him in accordance with the truth that is in Jesus. You were taught, with regard to your former way of life, to put off your old self, which is being corrupted by its deceitful desires to be made new in the attitude of your minds; and to put on the new self, created to be like God in true righteousness and holiness (Ephesians 4:17-24).

Did you live sexually pure today?
        Yes   *No*

Are you committed to staying sexually pure?
        Yes   *No*

DAY 3
Starter's Block

A Life of purity is a journey, a challenging journey. All journeys must have a starting point. All races begin at the starter's block. In order to pace ourselves, and know how far and from what direction we have come, we must know where we are starting.

Consider this:
But because of His great love for us, God, who is rich in mercy, made us alive with Christ even when we were dead in transgressions – it is by grace you have been saved (Ephesians 2:4-5).

Therefore if anyone is in Christ, he is a new creation; the old has gone, the new has come! (2 Corinthians 5:17).

The amazing part of these verses is the change that is described. In Ephesians it says that "we were dead, but God made us alive". In 2 Corinthians it describes how the old has gone and Christians are a "new creation." Noting the vast difference from the beginning to the end is cause for rejoicing and praise to God. So as we pursue purity, let's note at the beginning of our journey, that at the end we can rejoice in the amazing changes God has made in us!

Answer these questions as clearly as possible.

Question 1. What are your views and feelings right now about purity as a complete lifestyle?

Question 2. Who or what has helped form your views and feelings about purity?

Question 3. In regard to purity, what is your goal? What do you desire for your future?

Question 4. Write your own definition of purity.

Question 5. In what areas of your life do you want or need the most work?

Read this story about a life that was transformed by Jesus.

As he [Jesus] went along, he saw a man blind from birth. His disciples asked him, "Rabbi, who sinned, this man or his parents, that he was born blind?" "Neither this man nor his parents sinned," said Jesus, "but this happened so that the work of God might be displayed in his life. As long as it is day, we must do the work of him who sent me. Night is coming, when no one can work. While I am in the world, I am the light of the world."

Having said this, he spit on the ground, made some mud with the saliva and put it on the man's eyes. "Go", he told him, "Wash in the Pool of Siloam". So the man went and washed, and came home seeing.

His neighbors and those who had formerly seen him begging asked, "Isn't this the same man who used to sit and beg?" Some claimed he was. Others said. "No, he only looks like him." But he himself insisted, "I am the man."

Now the day on which Jesus had made the mud and opened the man's eyes was a Sabbath. Therefore the Pharisees also asked him how he had received his sight. "He put mud on my eyes," the man replied, "and I washed, and now I see." Some of the Pharisees said, "This man is not from God, for he does not keep the Sabbath." But others asked, "How can a sinner do such miraculous signs?" So they were divided.

The Jews still did not believe that he had been blind and had received his sight until they sent for the man's parents. "Is this your son?" they asked. Is this the one you say was born blind? How is it that now he can see?"

"We know he is our son," the parents answered, "and we know he was born blind. But how he can see now, or who opened his eyes, we don't know. Ask him. He is of age; he will speak for himself." His parents said this because they were afraid of the Jews, for already the Jews had decided that anyone who acknowledged that Jesus was the Christ would be put out of the synagogue.

A second time they summoned the man who had been blind. "Give glory to God," they said. "We know this man [Jesus] is a sinner." He replied, "Whether he is a sinner or not, I don't know. One thing I do know. I was blind but now I see!" (John 9:1-9,14-16,18-22,24-25).

Here is a radical story of a life that was changed because of the power of Jesus Christ. This man's ailment was physical. Many of our struggles are more internal struggles that are not so visible, but they are still sickness and ailment of heart. We still need Jesus to heal us. We can learn a lot from this man's response to his interaction with Jesus.

To begin, let's look at the starting point of this man. He was blind. He lived in total darkness and had never seen anything, because he was blind from birth. The man's story continued as he met Jesus who called himself "the Light of the world". Where the Light is, darkness cannot remain. Next, Jesus made some mud and touched directly on the man's weakest spot – the point of his ailment – his eyes. Then Jesus told him to go and wash himself. When he did, the Bible says his eyes were opened and he went home seeing. So what can we learn from this part of the story?

1. Jesus touched the man's blindness. Knowing your starting point, your "blindness", will affect you in amazing ways as Jesus touches that very spot in your life. Jesus didn't touch the man's arm or his leg; he spit and put mud directly on his eyes, the part that was broken. I'm sure it was uncomfortable to have Jesus touching him in a place that had been a source of embarrassment, frustration and maybe even anger his whole life. Yet he allowed Jesus to touch him there and he was never the same. Do you desire Jesus Himself to touch the weakest, darkest parts of you, and make you whole? That is the first question to ask yourself as you pursue purity.

2. Jesus gave the man some instructions. He told him to go wash himself. The blind man went and washed himself as Jesus asked, and the Bible says he went home seeing. Will you go and wash yourself when Jesus instructs you? Will you follow Jesus in cleansing the spots that Jesus tells you need cleaned? The Word of God is that which washes us clean, will you dive into it with gusto? That is the second question to ask yourself as you engage in this battle for purity.

3. Jesus changed the man's life. Look at the responses from others. No one believed him. They doubted he really was changed. Even the Pharisees called his parents to ask if he was really their son. When they finally asked the man directly about what happened, his answer was not theological or philosophical, it was simply a testimony of the change he had experienced in his life. He said, "...one thing I do know, I once was blind but now I see!" Wow. The power of a testimony of a changed life is something with which no one can argue. As you pursue and see victory in purity in your life, never underestimate the power of sharing your testimony with others. Simply stating what Jesus has changed in you will have profound impact.

That is why we looked at your starting point today. Jesus said the blind man was born blind so that "the work of God might be displayed in his life" (John 9:3). Your struggles with purity may also be used for a similar purpose. Yours can be a mighty 3-point testimony:
1. What I was
2. What happened when I met Jesus
3. What I am today
Share this with others!

Scripture to Consider

Whatever you do, work at it with all your heart, as working for the Lord, not for men (Colossians 3:23).

Did you live sexually pure today?
        Yes   No

Are you committed to staying sexually pure?
        Yes   No

DAY 4
Pure Gold

We want to give you a great picture of purity. We want you to get a glimpse of all the rewards and benefits involved in a pure life. Sure, you know it will be a big challenge, but the reason it is such a great challenge is because the rewards and blessings are so great!

Think about your ultimate dream for a relationship. It probably involves lasting commitment, enjoyment of each other, easy communication and more. It would not involve unfaithfulness, lack of trust, cruelty, pain, or loneliness. No one pursues a relationship looking for its destruction. The friendships you have made weren't formed knowing and planning for a painful ending.

So if we do not desire bitter endings of relationships, how do they happen so often? Maybe you know what I'm talking about because you have suffered through a divorce with your parents. Or maybe you, yourself, have suffered through a painful cut in a deep relationship. Whatever the case, it was not your ultimate desire for that relationship. Is it possible to be able to live out your ultimate dream relationship? Yes. There is no perfect person (except Jesus), so all relationships involving imperfect people will be imperfect. But all relationships do not have to end painfully and bitterly. There is a way to have your dream... the dream that God has written upon your heart when He created you; the dream of a relationship as precious as pure gold.

Question 1. Describe your dream relationship. Whether it's a husband or wife or best friend, describe it here:

Read this encouraging testimony from Cindy Mast: I never knew my "dream" relationship was actually possible. All my friends were married and even starting to have kids, but I was still alone. I prayed everyday that my hopes for my "dream" marriage would be fulfilled, but the Lord brought no men across my path that I would ever consider as

17

a possible marriage partner. See, I had set high standards for purity and I committed to pursue that in my own life, and in the life of someone I might marry. Finding men who valued purity as I did was difficult, if not impossible. Other Christians even told me I was "too picky". I was 26 and had to deliberately choose purity priorities every day. The testing was intense and daily. There were days when I doubted whether I would ever enjoy what my heart desired, and I was tempted to give in to pressures. The Lord continued to send friends my way to help me fight on and hold out hope for what the Lord had in store. A good friend once reminded me of Jesus' promise that "all these things" would be given to those who would "seek first His kingdom and His righteousness" (Matthew 6:33). So I continued to pray and seek God first, trusting that my hope in Him would not lead to disappointment.

Then one day I had a conversation that changed my life. It was a conversation with a guy I had known as a kid. We talked for over three hours. He was fun and interesting and his relationship with God was clearly evident. He was pursuing God and pursuing purity in his own life, and that made me want to pursue him! As we continued to talk and spend time together, we knew God had created us for each other. Within a year we were married! The Lord had answered my prayers, and I can't describe to you the joy, the peace, the energy that comes from pursuing God and His greatest desire for your life, whatever that may be. For me, the relationship I now enjoy with my husband is far more enjoyable and valuable than even the purest gold. God will never disappoint those who seek Him first! God has given me the man of my dreams and my best friend. He is definitely one of the biggest blessings of my life, and I can't imagine what my life would be missing without pursuing God first and His designs for me. Life and relationships that are full of peace, joy and security are just the tip of the iceberg of rewards for those who pursue God above every other thing.

The way to enjoy a relationship as precious as pure gold is through purity. Does this sound too simple? Elizabeth Elliot said it well: "I'm always having to explain to people that when I say there is a simple answer I do not necessarily mean there is an easy answer. It's easy enough to understand – in other words, it's simple. But doing it is just plain hard."[4] She's exactly right, there is a simple way to enjoy all the rewards and benefits of purity – just be pure. But doing purity is just plain hard! That's why this entire course is designed to teach and equip you in ways to do purity and live purely. Over all, we can teach you as much as possible, but the work will still be yours. God will be your continual strength and help, giving you grace to help you overcome. But purity will be a fight you must commit to and engage in day after day, even after this course ends.

So as you begin realizing the difficulty and challenge of a life of purity, let's first look at the amazing benefits; the rewards of a pure life. There are some physical and "earthly" benefits and some unbelievable "heavenly" rewards promised by the God of the universe.

Finally, brothers, whatever is true, whatever is noble, whatever is right, <u>whatever is pure</u>, whatever is lovely, whatever is admirable-if anything is excellent or praiseworthy-think about such things. Whatever you have learned or received or heard from me, or seen in me-put it into practice. And the God of peace will be with you (Philippians 4:8-9, emphasis ours).

Question 2. Who will be with you as the reward for thinking about pure things and all those other excellent things?

Question 3. As God is with you, what does he bring? The God of _____?

It is a truth of Scripture that *peace* follows *purity*. This, *this* is what we desire for you in your life; purity and the enjoyment of God's presence, and peace!

But the wisdom that comes from heaven is first of all pure; then peace-loving, considerate, submissive, full of mercy and good fruit, impartial and sincere (James 3:17).

Question 4. Wisdom from heaven is first of all what?

Blessed are the pure in heart, for they will see God (Matthew 5:8).

Question 5. What is the reward for the pure in heart?

Setting Captives Free teaches that "purity precedes perception." That is, if you want to see clearly, you must remove all impurity. Matthew 5:8 teaches this truth (as do a number of other Scriptures) when it says, "blessed are the pure in heart, for they will see God." Purity precedes perception.

The goal of this command is love, which comes from a pure heart and a good conscience and a sincere faith (1 Timothy 1:4-5).

Question 6. What comes from a pure heart?

I did not see a temple in the city, because the Lord God Almighty and the Lamb are its temple. The city does not need the sun or the moon to shine on it, for the glory of God gives it light, and the Lamb is its lamp. The nations will walk by its light, and the kings of the earth will bring their splendor into it. On no day will its gates ever be shut, for there will be no night there. The glory and honor of the nations will be brought into it. Nothing impure will ever enter it, nor will anyone who does what is shameful or deceitful, but only those whose names are written in the Lamb's book of life (Revelations 21:22-27).

Question 7. From the verses above, describe the future place where the "pure", whose names are written in the Lamb's book of life, will live.

Do not be afraid of what you are about to suffer. I tell you, the devil will put some of you in prison to test you, and you will suffer persecution for ten days. Be faithful, even to the point of death, and I will give you the crown of life (Revelation 2:10).

Pursuing purity is a battle. But do not be afraid of what you are suffering already or about to suffer. If you are faithful, do you know what Christ will give you in the end? According to Revelation 2:10b, He says, *"Be faithful, even to the point of death, and I will give you the crown of life"*. A crown of life! Not a Burger King Crown, not even the Crown Jewels of England, but the Crown of Life! You will experience life to the fullest and it will be given as a reward for you to wear as a crown on your head. Then the further reward will be to have such a gift, and be able to give that special gift back to Jesus in love and honor.

Okay, so those are just a few of the "heavenly" rewards and promises of God for a pure life. Peace, wisdom, seeing God, love, and the promise of Heaven are gifts from God as a result of purity. Those promises are greater than our simple minds can even comprehend. They far outweigh any earthly reward for purity. But since we are living here on earth right now and it is not always easy to grasp the immensity of the "heavenly" rewards, let's list some practical earthly rewards for purity. As we progress further in this course, we will get more in-depth with these blessings. But for now, imagine all these are yours for the enjoying...

1. Secure, blessed, trusting, and peaceful relationships
2. Life free from guilt, shame or regret
3. Life free from consequences of impurity
4. Greater capacity to love and be loved
5. Open communication with God

Question 8. Which reward(s) listed above stands out to you most? Why?

Question 9. Do you know that all these rewards/blessings can be yours – if you have a relationship with Jesus Christ?

Scripture to Consider

The LORD is near to all who call on him, to all who call on him in truth. He fulfills the desires of those who fear him; he hears their cry and saves them. The LORD watches over all who love him, but all the wicked he will destroy. My mouth will speak in praise of the LORD. Let every creature praise his holy name forever and ever (Psalm 145:18-21).

Did you live sexually pure today?
      Yes   *No*

Are you committed to staying sexually pure?
      Yes   *No*

Notes

DAY 5

Reality vs. Illusion

One of the main keys to overcoming sexual sin or any other sin keeping you impure is to learn to recognize **reality vs. illusion**. The Evil One gives us an enticing, seemingly harmless, picture of sin and we are drawn to it; we sense its enjoyment and any consequences look pale in comparison to the present fun it could be. Beware of that illusion! Webster's Dictionary defines illusion as
      1. a false idea or mistaken belief;
      2. the appearance of something that makes one see it in a false way.[5]
Illusions are not truth; they are lies. John 8:44 says about the Evil One, "…he was a murderer from the beginning, not holding to the truth, for there is no truth in him. When he lies, he speaks his native language, for he is a liar and the father of lies." Satan is the producer of lies and illusion! Therefore everything he offers you, although it sounds nice, is a lie. His intention is your disobedience to God and your destruction.

In order to survive Satan's continual attack, we must learn to <u>see</u> and <u>love</u> **reality** and not allow our lives to be captivated by an illusion that will fade and leave us empty. **Reality** is simply God's Truth; **illusion** is Satan's lie. Reality is found in God's Word; illusion is found in many other places that are apart from God's Word. Reality is the truth that God created you for a purpose. He loves you, desires your eternal happiness, and has an amazing plan for your life. Illusion is anything that tells us we have no purpose in life, sin won't harm us, God doesn't care about our happiness, or God is not in control of the circumstances in our lives. Think of popular movies, music, TV shows, and video games. Do they always show you truth and reality? Do they lead you to pursue a life of reality or a life of illusion? That is a question you must learn to ask yourself constantly.

We (Nathan and Jena) enjoy Christmas movies. There are funny ones about Santa Claus, snowmen or even elves. There are also cartoon movies about Rudolph or the *Grinch Who Stole Christmas*. But, if we don't know what reality is – that snowmen don't dance and reindeer can't fly – then we won't see and understand when we are shown illusions. Children don't have a full understanding of reality vs. illusion. They think Barney and Winnie the Pooh are real citizens in the community. Do you think that? No way! As we move from childhood toward adulthood our understanding of reality also grows! Because of that, now is the time to begin seeing the reality of purity and how it affects your life now and in the future.

One of the ways to know if you understand something is to explain it in your own words.

Question 1. What do we mean when we say "reality"?

Question 2. What is meant by "illusion"?

Remember, the Evil One will want to distract you with illusion – fake, temporary substitutes for reality. You cannot live a total life of illusion because reality always comes into your life at some point. So either we choose a life of reality now, in light of God and his Word, or we take our chances with illusion until reality hits us later with broken relationships, broken families and broken lives. You can't escape reality. Notice the root word in reality is <u>real</u>. We will always, ultimately, encounter reality. Will you choose it? If not, the consequences of illusion will quickly and sometimes painfully bring you back to reality.

Let's use pre-marital sex as an example. Reality is that it's a real temptation with real consequences. Reality is that God wants you to wait until you are married before you enjoy sex. Reality is knowing you need support and God's help to stay pure. Then what is illusion? In this case, illusion is a belief that pre-marital sex doesn't have consequences for everyone. Illusion is a belief that God only wants us to be unhappy and have no fun. Illusion is thinking that someone will finally love us if we have sex with them. See the pattern? If you start believing the illusion instead of living in reality, you are playing with fire and setting yourself up for hurtful reality to follow. Remember, we will always encounter reality at some point. For some in this scenario, that hurtful reality may be an unplanned baby, a sexually transmitted disease, a broken heart, a ruined reputation or even struggles later in your future marriage. Numbers 32:23 says, "But if you fail to do this, (follow God's commands) you will be sinning against the LORD; and you may be sure that your sin will find you out" (Explanation added).

The following testimony is from Michael: When I had gotten into pornography, I thought nothing of it. The information in it was kept from me. One night, I was going to stay the night with my friend. So what did I do? I brought my pictures with me. When I got to his house and started looking through my pictures, I noticed that one of my pictures had fallen out of my stack. I had to go to my house that same night because I forgot some clothes for the next night. When I looked in the toy room, I noticed that my dad was looking through my folders and he was listening to my music. That told me that he had found that missing picture. God had a role in this. He was the one that made that picture fall out of my stack. He did that because he does not like people doing that, so he showed it to my dad. Then my dad talked to me about what would really happen if I didn't stop.

You have a choice to make whether to live in light of God and His reality for eternity or in temporary illusion until God uses pain and struggle to eventually bring you back into reality.

Know this: This is reality… there is only **one true, thoroughly realistic guide to purity and sexuality,** and that is the Word of God! Anything outside of that is illusion and only leads to broken lives, broken marriages, broken relationships, and especially a broken relationship with your Heavenly Father! Maybe you aren't comfortable talking about sex, or haven't thought much about it or don't think you've been affected by it. That's okay. But understand that sexuality needs to be addressed and you need to make a commitment to purity in your life. **You can't just hope purity will happen.** We want to help you learn and understand the vital, wonderful, part God created within us called sexuality and the **real** way to protect that through purity.

Question 3. Do you think your view of sexuality and purity is based on the reality of God that you have learned or other illusions that have influenced you? Why?

Next, please read and think through the following Bible verses, then answer the questions below with your thoughts.

"Flee from sexual immorality. All other sins a man commits are outside his body, but he who sins sexually sins against his own body. Do you not know that your body is a temple of the Holy Spirit, who is in you, whom you have received from God? You are not your own; you were bought at a price. Therefore honor God with your body" (1 Corinthians 6:18-20).

Question 5. According to the above verses, what is the reality about our bodies?

Question 6. What illusions can popular culture lead us to believe about our bodies?

The following testimony is from Scott: One night I was using a search engine to look for pornography. I typed in "porn" and at the same time I was praying for God's forgiveness and for Him to help me. This website (Setting Captives Free.com) popped up and I immediately signed up for Purity Challenge. Over the last thirty days, I have grown closer to God and have learned how to deal with temptation. I have made a lot of changes, like I am not getting on the computer after 9 PM and I have to be in bed by 10:30 PM because I am most tempted and not thinking clearly during the late-night hours. I have also learned during this course that the feeling we get from sexual images is all an illusion from Satan. He wants us all to think that that's what we really want and that it will fulfill us, but the truth is, we can search all night long into the morning hours looking for the perfect image and we never find it. We just keep on searching, and we want more. We are never, ever satisfied. Then, afterwards, we have a hollow feeling and we can even get a disgusted feeling with ourselves and the rest of the day is ruined. With Jesus, though, we can go to sleep at night and be completely satisfied because we know Him and we know there is no other. There is no image that compares to Him. He is God and he fulfills us in every way. I am getting stronger every day and I pray that everyone taking this course will know they aren't alone.

Scripture to Consider

O LORD, you have searched me and you know me. You know when I sit and when I rise; you perceive my thoughts from afar. You discern my going out and my lying down; you are familiar with all my ways. Before a word is on my tongue you know it completely, O LORD. You hem me in, behind and before; you have laid your hand upon me. Such knowledge is too wonderful for me, too lofty for me to attain. Where can I go from your Spirit? Where can I flee from your presence? If I go up to the heavens, you are there; if I make my bed in the depths, you are there. If I rise on the wings of the dawn, if I settle on the far side of the sea, even there your hand will guide me; your right hand will hold me fast. If I say, 'Surely the darkness will hide me and the light become night around me,' even the darkness will not be dark to you; the night will shine like the day, for darkness is as light to you. For you created my inmost being; you knit me together in my mother's womb. I praise you because I am fearfully and wonderfully made; your works are wonderful, I know that full well. My frame was not hidden from you when I was made in the secret place. When I was woven together in the depths of the earth, your eyes saw my unformed body. All the days ordained for me were written in your book before one of them came to be. How precious to me are your thoughts, O God! How vast is the sum of them! Were I to count them, they would outnumber the grains of sand. When I awake, I am still with you (Psalm 139).

Did you live sexually pure today?
    Yes   *No*

Are you committed to staying sexually pure?
    Yes   *No*

Notes

DAY 6
Who You Know

Let's begin with the following testimony from Chris:

> My testimony starts a few years back just before my father died. To make a long story short, he was very verbally abusive to me, inflicting much pain on me and caused me to inflict many wounds on myself through lack of confidence. Near the end, I just didn't care about my life anymore. I felt so tormented inside, wondering where God was, not wanting to live. This is the time in my life when Satan grabbed hold of me and caused me to fall into pornography. When I was a mere child he planted seeds in me that grew into a monstrous lust as I grew older. I was so young I didn't know how to combat it. I always knew that pornography was wrong, I always hated myself for giving in, but I felt like I couldn't tell anyone. I knew that if I told my father he would have just yelled at me and made me feel like the scum of the earth once again. Then God did something I didn't expect—He took my father home. I was the one to find him dead. Strangely enough, losing him struck no emotion in me. I loved my father, but losing him was like a weight off my shoulders, especially when I look back now. This set him free and started to set me free. Soon after this event, my pain reached an all-time high; I couldn't stand it anymore. I found myself crying out to God, wondering why He didn't answer me. Then it hit me—I wasn't truly saved. I prayed the best I knew how and asked Christ into my life, and I haven't been the same since. He's helped me get rid of all the impurities in my life and He's helping me get over the loss of my dad and also to control my lust now after years of hopeless fighting. Thanks to His grace and the teachings in this course, I now know what true freedom really is.

As with other things in life, it's not **what** we know but **who** we know that makes the difference. That same truth applies in your pursuit of purity. **Who** we know and are connected to is the key! We have all tried to stay "good," to stay "clean," but we all mess up! The Bible says, "For all have sinned and fall short of the glory of God" (Romans 3:23). So how can you ever succeed in a battle for purity if you're already born a sinner? Good question. Here's the answer...

It's all about **WHO** we know. Jesus Christ is the only Son of God. He is perfect. He is completely pure and without sin. From the days of Adam, every human being born on the earth is a sinner. We are imperfect, impure and full of sin. There is no way we can approach or have a relationship with a totally pure

God and King apart from some kind of mediator! To pay for our sin ourselves would be death and being separated from God forever. But this is where the most amazing sacrifice happened. God knew we could never pay for our own sins. We could never conquer the death and the evil that ensnares us. So God sent Jesus Christ, His perfect Son, to take the punishment of our sins and pay the price we should have paid. He was totally pure and innocent, yet He became our sin and was killed and punished. Jesus, being God, is very different from us. After three days in the tomb, Jesus Christ rose from the dead, proving once and for all His power over sin and death! Now, because Jesus has already paid for our sin, we can no longer be held responsible to pay for those sins. Now we can be completely clean and have full access to a pure, Holy God and the life and strength He offers us! But this is only possible through a relationship with Jesus.

Question 1. If Jesus were to walk into the room in which you are sitting right now, would you jump up and be glad to see Him? Or would you quickly think of all the things you should straighten out before you feel comfortable talking to Him? How would you respond?

In order to be connected rightly to God, we must see our need for Jesus' death to take the place of what we really deserve. We must be covered and claimed by His payment on the cross. We cannot get to God apart from connecting what Jesus did and who He is to ourselves personally. A relationship with Jesus Christ secures our eternity in heaven with God because then when He looks at us He sees Jesus Christ. And that makes us sons and daughters of God! He is our heavenly Father! Jesus Christ is **WHO** we must know to have any power and victory in this battle for a pure life.

Question 2. Do you know Jesus Christ as your personal Savior? Please explain.

A few hundred years ago there lived a young man who was tired of hearing about God from his mother and grandmother. He decided to reject what they had been trying to teach him and began indulging in the world's pleasures. He got so deep into sin that he no longer wanted to have anything to do with God. His final attempt to rid himself of the nagging guilt was to join a band of sailors and head off to sea on a merchant ship. It was during a violent storm in the middle of the ocean that this man realized that no matter how far he ran, God would not let him go. He accepted God's payment for all the sins he had committed and became a true child of the King right there in the belly of the ship. Later he wrote a poem that described his ordeal, and maybe yours. You might recognize it.

Amazing grace how sweet the sound
That saved a wretch like me.
I once was lost but now am found,
Was blind, but now I see.

'Twas grace that taught my heart to fear
And grace my fears relieved.
How precious did that grace appear
The hour I first believed.

John Newton realized that it was only the grace of Jesus Christ that could open his eyes and give him life and hope.

The more we get to know Jesus, the more we learn about the power that is able to fight and win over sin and temptation in our lives. Often we don't connect with Jesus; we don't spend time getting to know Him because we have a wrong perception of Him. Some old paintings depict Jesus as a weak, sad creature living in days long ago. What we don't see is that He is alive right now! He knows your name and everything about you. He is so powerful that no sin or even death could win over Him! He is the kind of loving, yet all-powerful ally you must have on your side! Let's talk about some true qualities of Jesus.

Read the following verses and answer these questions.

The Son is the radiance of God's glory and the exact representation of His being, sustaining all things by His powerful Word. After He had provided purification for sins, He sat down at the right hand of the Majesty in heaven (Hebrews 1:3).

You have made known to me the path of life, you will fill me with joy in your presence, with eternal pleasures at your right hand (Psalm 16:11).

Question 3. According to Hebrews 1:3, <u>who</u> is at the right hand of God?
    A. Bodyguard
    B. The Son, Jesus
    C. Michael, the angel
Question 4. According to Psalm 16:11, <u>what</u> is at the right hand of God?
    A. Eternal pleasures
    B. Streets of gold
    C. The Apostles

Question 5. Can you find the connection? Where (or in Whom) can you find eternal pleasures?

Do you see it? The connection, I mean? Psalm 16:11 tells us that there are "pleasures" at the right hand of God, and Hebrews 1:3 tells us that Jesus is at the right hand of God. Clearly Jesus Christ can become our greatest Pleasure in life.

Through him all things were made; without him nothing was made that has been made. In him was life, and that life was the light of men. The light shines in the darkness, but the darkness has not understood it (John 1:3-5).

Question 6. What are some qualities of Jesus described in this verse?

When Jesus saw their faith, he said, "Friend, your sins are forgiven" (Luke 5:20).

Question 7. What does Jesus have the ability to do? What name does He call the man?

While Jesus was having dinner at Levi's house, many tax collectors and 'sinners' were eating with him and his disciples, for there were many who followed him. When the teachers of the law who were Pharisees saw him eating with the 'sinners' and tax collectors, they asked his disciples: "Why does he eat with tax collectors and 'sinners'?"   On hearing this, Jesus said to them, "It is not the healthy who need a doctor, but the sick. I have not come to call the righteous, but sinners" (Mark 2:15-17).

Question 8. What picture does this verse give you? What is Jesus' desire?

It is our greatest desire to see you captivated by Jesus Christ above all. When your heart is fascinated with Him, then lust, impure thoughts and actions cannot remain. *John 1:5* in "The Message" says, "The Life-Light blazed out of the darkness; the darkness couldn't put it out." Jesus Christ is the "Life-Light" and wherever He is all darkness and sin must flee! This is the Person to know as you fight to pursue purity.

> **Course member Roxanne writes:** Up until I was 11 I thought that I was a good kid and didn't get into too much trouble. My parents were Christians and always took me to church, so I thought I was all right. One Sunday morning I began to let what I had been taught by my parents and others sink in. I realized I was not all right! I was a sinner and I wasn't going to heaven! I remembered what Christ did for me. He died on the cross for my sins. Christ loved me so much that He went through torture and death to save me. That broke my heart! I prayed to God and asked forgiveness for my sins. I also accepted Jesus as Lord and Savior over my life. Since I was saved, I've had ups and downs. There were times when I was peaceful and happy. Then there were times when my flesh took over and I was angry or jealous. I've had to go back and ask forgiveness so many times I've lost count! What gives me peace is knowing what Jesus did for me and others. Jesus is the One who is helping me stop sinning, or help me get through troubles. I may have family, but Jesus is the only One who can really help me.

Scripture to Consider

But because of his great love for us, God, who is rich in mercy, made us alive with Christ even when we were dead in transgressions–it is by grace you have been saved. And God raised us up with Christ and seated us with him in the heavenly realms in Christ Jesus, in order that in the coming ages he might show the incomparable riches of his grace, expressed in his kindness to us in Christ Jesus. For it is by grace you have been saved, through faith–and this not from yourselves, it is the gift of God- not by works, so that no one can boast (Ephesians 2:4-10).

Did you live sexually pure today?
  Yes   *No*

Are you committed to staying sexually pure?
  Yes   *No*

DAY 7
Who You Are

In the Disney movie "The Lion King" there is one scene that sticks out from the others. This scene occurs near the end of the movie. Simba's father had died, and because Simba believed his father's death was his fault, he ran away. Simba left his royal duty as the heir, which was to take his father's place as king. He ran away and hid with a pig and some other strange animal. In his absence, the Prideland fell into bad hands and was being destroyed. No one thought Simba was alive so no one had hope of saving the Prideland from its enemies. Then one day, a "wise" monkey found Simba. He told him he knew his father. Of course, Simba, weighed down by discouragement and guilt wanted to find his father to get his wisdom on things. When the monkey finally led Simba to the place where he was to meet his father, it was a pool of water and Simba saw his own reflection, which looked just like his father. At the same time, he heard his father's voice saying, *"Simba, you have forgotten me."* Simba replied, *"No Father, I would never forget you."* His father said, *"You have forgotten who you are and therefore have forgotten me. You are my son...*He reminds Simba, *"Remember who you are. Remember who you are."*[6]

Question 1. Do you know who you are? How would you describe yourself to someone else?

Today, we're going to talk about a very important part of reality—knowing who you are. If you truly know Christ as your Savior then your whole identity has changed from when you were an unbeliever, outside of Christ. It is now connected to Christ and knowing who He is, first through a relationship with him (as we talked about yesterday), and second through daily being made more like Him. Knowing who <u>He</u> is, is key to knowing who <u>*you*</u> are!

You Are a Justified Sinner

We are all sinners at birth. We are born spiritually dead in our sin and only through Jesus Christ reaching out to us and breathing life into our spirits do we truly become "alive". Our eyes are opened to our sinfulness, our desperation, and our need for a Savior. For some, that happens at a young age, for some it happens later in life. Whenever it happens, Christ penetrates our lives, redeems us from death and declares the sinner "justified". But what does "justified" mean? One old country pastor said it this way, "Just (as) if I'd never sinned." The dictionary says it means "to be freed from blame or guilt". So when Christ becomes our Savior, He saves us from the blame and guilt we deserve because of our sin. At the moment we accept Jesus Christ as our Savior we are "justified", and our whole identity changes. The core of who we are, our identity, is no longer tied to sin and death, but to Jesus Christ and life! Knowing who we really are at our core, the center of our person, where Jesus resides and has given us life, is vital to the daily battle against sin in our lives and pursuing a pure life.

Pastor and author John Piper states that knowing who we are is an important part of our battle with sin. He said, "The secret of rugged joy in the battle with sin is to fight to become what we are in Christ. You have already *died* with Christ (Romans 6:5-6); therefore "consider yourselves dead to sin and alive to God in Christ Jesus" (Romans 6:11). You have already been *made alive* together with Christ (Ephesians 2:5); therefore, "seek the things that are above" (Colossians 3:1). You are already *holy* in Christ (Colossians 3:12); therefore "be holy in all your conduct" (1 Peter 1:15). You *already* are the light of the world in Christ (Matthew 5:14); therefore, "let your light shine" (Matthew 5:16). Fight for joy, not by doing things that establish your identity with God, but by becoming what your identity already is with God in Christ. Become what you are."[7]

Question 2. Explain the difference between doing things to try to establish who you are, and simply knowing and being who you are.

Look at Ephesians 2: 4-6,19: But because of his great love for us, God, who is rich in mercy, made us alive with Christ even when we were dead in transgressions—it is by grace you have been saved. And God raised us up with Christ and seated us with him in the heavenly realms in Christ Jesus… Consequently, you are no longer foreigners and aliens, but fellow citizens with God's people and members of God's household.

You Are an Heir

Let me show you the implications of this. As long as the heir is a minor, he has no advantage over the slave. Though legally he owns the entire inheritance, he is subject to tutors and administrators until whatever day the father has set for emancipation. That is the way it is with us: When we were minors, we were just like slaves ordered around by simple instructions (the tutors and administrators of this world), with no say in the conduct of our own lives. But when the time set by God the Father arrived, God sent his Son, born among us of a woman, born under the conditions of the law so that he might redeem those of us who have been kidnapped by the law. Thus we have been set free to experience our rightful heritage.

You can tell for sure that you are now fully adopted as his own children because God sent the Spirit of his Son into our lives crying out, "Papa! Father!" Doesn't that privilege of intimate conversation with God make it plain that you are not a slave, but a child? And if you are a child, you're also an heir, with complete access to the inheritance (Galatians 4:1-7, *"The Message"*).

What is an heir? Think of the many movies you've seen with a king or queen in it. To what is an "heir" entitled? An heir is a person who has the rights to property or title after the owner has died. Other words that have similar meaning are: successor, beneficiary, recipient. The Apostle Paul's concept of a spiritual inheritance for Christians or being an "heir" was influenced by Jewish, Greek and Roman practices. Three pictures of these influences were: (1) inheritance was regarded as immediate as well as ultimate, (2) all legitimate heirs usually shared the inheritance equally and jointly rather than a division favoring a firstborn son, and (3) legally adopted children enjoyed full inheritance rights along with natural offspring.[8] Being adopted carried just as much weight as a natural born heir. That holds great news for us! Look at this verse:

For he chose us in him before the creation of the world to be holy and blameless in his sight. In love he predestined us to be adopted as his sons through Jesus Christ, in accordance with his pleasure and will-to the praise of his glorious grace, which he has freely given us in the One he loves (Ephesians 1:4-6).

Consider this:

Now if we are children, then we are heirs; heirs of God and co-heirs with Christ, if indeed we share in his sufferings in order that we may also share in his glory (Romans 8:17).

Question 3. What are your thoughts about being heirs of God? How does that affect the way you see yourself? Explain

You Are a Value-Bearer

Really knowing who we are can only come from knowing our value in Jesus Christ.

As Humans...

Humans are the only creation that bears the image of God "Then God said, "Let us make man in our image, in our likeness, and let them rule over the fish of the sea and the birds of the air, over the livestock, over all the earth, and over all the creatures that move along the ground. So God created man in his own image, in the image of God he created him; male and female he created them" (Genesis 1:26-27). We are different from the trees and animals in that we, as humans, were created in the image of God. That is a value and honor given to us by our Creator at the very beginning. Whether people acknowledge God in their lives or not, no one can deny that we, as humans, are valued above all creation because of the image of God stamped on us at creation. (Of course bearing that image does not give us salvation, because sin has marred that image in us and our good works are as "filthy rags" (Isaiah 64:6) apart from Jesus Christ.)

As Christians...

As Christians, Jesus Christ lives in us. He is the most valuable thing about us. Christ gives us value when He makes His home within the deepest parts of the heart and soul. Our true value cannot be felt, understood or lived apart from Christ! We don't need to look to surroundings, people or performances to find our worth, but our worth can be found as we look to Jesus Christ and His sacrifice to have a relationship with us! He suffered and died on the cross in order to forgive our sins and give us eternal life. He has made us new creatures, and that is who we are! As Jesus Christ lives in us, he gives us new value.

Question 4. Do you believe that you, as a child and heir of God, and as a justified sinner have extreme value? Where does that value come from? Explain your answer.

Declared Identity vs. Challenged Identity

Author Paula Rinehart writes, "It is good to remember that God's word comes to us in straight forward declarations about who we are and how he sees us in Christ. You are a child of God, redeemed by the blood of Christ, lavished by his grace. You are. You are. You just are—because God <u>declares</u> you are. There is nothing to do but lay claim to who you are in Christ. But the enemy of our souls comes to us in a different manner, amazingly similar to the way he came to Jesus in the wilderness. Do you remember how he talked to Christ? "If you are the Son of God, command that these stones become bread" (Matthew 4:3). *If you are*... that is the key phrase. The enemy <u>challenges</u> us at the bedrock level of our identities. He says that who we are is not something to rest in and thank God for. Instead, he suggests that it is something to be proved over and over. *If you are*..."[9]

How can you know God's view of you—your identity in Him? Spend some time talking to God and reading his Word today, while asking God to show you who you <u>truly</u> are – who He has declared you to be. His answer to you is Truth and He will show you who you really are because of Christ. Knowing God's view of you is vital to living daily as a pure, new creation.

Course member Caila writes: I am the typical nice girl who wanted to please God in every way I could. But I had a few things I was struggling with and I knew I must get rid of them. I was struggling with areas in sexual purity. But little did I know how sexual sin was so controlling. I knew this was wrong, so I tried with all my might to get out of it myself! Where was God in all this? He was nowhere and I was getting nowhere. As the days went by, I kept drifting from God and His Living Water. It seemed like I wasn't getting through to Him at all. Searching on the Internet, I came across the site, settingcaptivesfree.com. I totally believe this was God-sent!

Everyday I did the lessons and I learned that I can't be a slave to sin and to righteousness all at the same time! I learned my royalty in God and how much He loves me and that made me think why would I want sin in my body when God lives in it. Through these lessons and the power of God, He altered my mind about my pursuit of purity and He let me know that Jesus already died on the cross for my sins and that I have already been forgiven! I've got the power with Him (not on my own) to say "No" to sexual temptation. God gave me the equipment I need to make a battle plan. When temptation strikes I will sing worship songs, I will read the Bible and I will pray. The enemy has no stronghold in my mind anymore. However, I would be wrong to say that I am completely free, since purity is a life-long struggle, but I now have the courage to walk away from sin and turn to God forever. I want to delight in the Lord so I may experience His wonderful blessings and promises that He has for my life. I am a new person in Christ now!

Your pursuit of purity is evidence of how clearly you understand God's view of you – who you truly are. Your pursuit of purity should be fueled by this understanding of the extreme value God places on your body, heart and soul. To truly know who you are, you must remember whose you are! If you have a relationship with Jesus Christ, you are justified, you have value to Him, and you are an heir of God with a future that will be beyond imagination! The practicalities of pure living will fall in line a bit easier if you can truly grasp your identity and value in Christ!

Question 5. If you were to pay a high price for a one-of-a-kind shirt, say a jersey actually worn by Michael Jordan, or a dress worn by Princess Diana, how would you treat it? (Throw it on the floor? Spill stuff on it? Wash the car in it?) How would you let your friends treat it? How does this connect to living purely?

Question 6. To you, what is the most encouraging thought from the lesson today? (See this as encouragement from God's heart to yours!)

Scripture to Consider

But because of his great love for us, God, who is rich in mercy, made us alive with Christ even when we were dead in transgressions-it is by grace you have been saved. And God raised us up with Christ and seated us with him in the heavenly realms in Christ Jesus, in order that in the coming ages he might show the incomparable riches of his grace, expressed in his kindness to us in Christ Jesus. For it is by grace you have been saved, through faith-and this not from yourselves, it is the gift of God- not by works, so that no one can boast. For we are God's workmanship, created in Christ Jesus to do good works, which God prepared in advance for us to do (Ephesians 2:4-10).

Did you live sexually pure today?
        Yes   *No*

Are you committed to staying sexually pure?
        Yes   *No*

Notes

DAY 8
Reality of Those Hormones!

In this lesson as well as the next few lessons, we will look into some important issues in teenage life and their effect on purity. Today we will look at adolescence itself, and see how you can use this important, crazy time in your life to set the stage for a lifetime of purity.

What makes adolescence vastly different from other stages of life is the onset of hormones! After a dozen or so years on this planet, the human body goes through a radical series of changes. Glands suddenly kick in and start producing larger quantities of hormones. These hormones in turn produce physical changes in the body. It is during this time that the differences between male and female become more apparent, and these differences become more appealing to the opposite gender. Thus begins the formation of our sexuality as humans. These sudden changes can produce various emotions and reactions in us ranging from excitement and wonder to anxiety and even depression.

The movie "The Sandlot" gives us a funny picture of hormones! One kid, "Squints", has just bought a baseball with his friend and is on his way to play when he is stopped dead in his tracks by the sight of a beautiful girl. He stands there with his mouth hanging open at merely the sight of "Wendy Peffercorn" walking down the street. She's a lifeguard, a few years older, and he's "swooning" as all his buddies tease him. Instead of playing baseball, all he can think about is Wendy. Later that day, as all the boys are splashing around at the community pool, Squints' crush on Wendy leads him to make his move, as only a crazy young boy would do. As Wendy sits above the pool in her lifeguard chair, Squints jumps off the diving board, sinks to the bottom of the pool and fakes drowning so Wendy will use her lifeguard skills to rescue him. Wendy jumps in, pulls him from the water and as he lays there limp on the concrete, Wendy tries desperately to revive him by using CPR. Squints lays there motionless on the concrete until finally he seizes his big moment, and to Wendy's surprise, wraps his arms around her and plants a big kiss on her mouth! A kid in love! That little stunt got him kicked out of the local pool for the entire summer, but it's a great picture of crazy hormones![10]

The important thing to realize is that there is nothing evil or ungodly associated with adolescence! There is nothing evil or ungodly about our hormones! Our hormones cannot make us sin. They are a gift of God! All of these changes are signs of passing from one stage to another – from child to adult. It is how God has designed the human body, and there should be no shame in that. It's God's great design! Go ahead and thank Him for it!

Sure, most of this is textbook information you can get in any health class. But knowing that these changes are going on, as heirs of God, how should we view and deal with our hormones? First let's look at how one of the Psalmists tells us to view our bodies, and then we'll look at some practical tips for dealing with our hormones. Read the following Scripture and answer the questions that follow.

For you created my inmost being; you knit me together in my mother's womb. I praise you because I am fearfully and wonderfully made; your works are wonderful, I know that full well. My frame was not hidden from you when I was made in the secret place. When I was woven together in the depths of the earth, your eyes saw my unformed body. All the days ordained for me were written in your book before one of them came to be (Psalm 139:13-16).

Question 1. In the beginning of the verse above, the writer states that he will praise God. Why?

Question 2. From the verse above, the works of God are:
   A. Funny
   B. Boring
   C. Marvelous
   D. Rare

Question 3. According to the verses above, what did God see?

Question 4. Before we were formed, what was written in God's book?

Question 5. What further comments do you have on this verse? How does this affect the way you see yourself in this adolescent stage?

I hope you can see in this Scripture some valuable points that you can take hold of as you struggle and press through this challenging time of life. In the verses above we see that we are "fearfully and wonderfully made." Our bodies are not just walking heaps of amino acids, carbohydrates, sugars and fats. We were carefully constructed, "made in the secret place... woven together in the depths of the earth." Puberty and adolescence are components of this magnificent creation.

Here is a question for thought. Does it seem as if your hormones, at least sometimes, are fighting against your desire for purity? You may wonder, "How do raging hormones and required purity ever let a person live in peace?" Great question! Okay, know this: for a teenager, **hormones now** are gifts created for a **future, God-blessed enjoyment and purpose**; and **purity now** is also vital for that **future, God-blessed enjoyment and purpose.** So the two are not actually enemies! They work together in God's amazing plan! For successful, fulfilled sexuality in God's plan, you must have both hormones and purity working together! Hormones without purity to keep them in check are dangerous and destructive. And if there are no hormones, is there even a struggle for purity?

Obviously, God will take care of developing the hormones but you are responsible to seek God and do everything possible to pursue the purity that's needed for a blessed future. Ok, so let's get practical for a few minutes. You have all these raging hormones, your body is in a state of chaos, your sex drive and emotions are going from zero to hyper drive, and there is nothing you can do about it until it all ends, right? Well, not exactly. The following points are some ideas on how to calm or redirect those raging hormones, and protect your purity. Remember, these won't take the hormones away, (because we don't want to take them away), but they are good suggestions to help you redirect your valuable energy as you pursue purity.

1. **Pour your energy into deepening & strengthening your relationship with God. You can't pursue Him hard enough!**
   - **Seek God** for His strength and grace to understand and withstand the sexual urges in you.

45

- **Read the Bible** and learn about Who God is and His purposes for you!
- **Memorize verses**. Write them on post-its and stick them in your car, on your mirror, in your wallet… Soak yourself in the reality of God and His Words to <u>you</u>.
- **Pray and Praise lots.** Pray that He would keep you from temptation and protect you in temptation. <u>Pray</u> tons and <u>praise</u> Him tons for what He has in store for you.

2. **Pour your energy into activities, service for others, and ministry for the Lord. Re-channel your drive into service and hard work.**
    - Actively work to **meet needs of people** around you instead of pleasing yourself. Is someone you know hurting? Can you help? Can you fix something for someone or do jobs outside to help them?
    - Get involved with **active groups** of people that have similar goals and desires as you do and work to accomplish something together…prayer groups, youth groups…
    - Find ways to **be influential and help teach** someone younger than you the need for purity and pursuing God above other stuff. Teach what you're learning!
    - **Make a promise** not to look at or think about things that will not help you conquer sin. Find a close friend or two to ask you how you're doing with that.
    - **If there's still energy left, go for a run or a good workout!** (You won't have as much energy left to get in trouble!)

3. **Find a friend you trust to hold you accountable and encourage you toward purity. Alone we are easily conquered, but "a chord of three strands isn't quickly broken " (Ecclesiastes 4:12).**

Question 6. Please record how you will implement these ideas in your life to help preserve your purity.

Do you realize the **reality** of the way God made you, hormones and all? Do you understand that what God creates is always good, but only in His designed context and timing? Is it clear how your pursuit of purity must match the intensity of the hormones raging? Remember that you can't just hope purity will happen.

Scripture to Consider

In you, O LORD, I have taken refuge; let me never be put to shame. Rescue me and deliver me in your righteousness; turn your ear to me and save me. Be my rock of refuge, to which I can always go; give the command to save me, for you are my rock and my fortress. Deliver me, O my God, from the hand of the wicked, from the grasp of evil and cruel men. For you have been my hope, O Sovereign LORD, my confidence since my youth. From birth I have relied on you; you brought me forth from my mother's womb. I will ever praise you (Psalm 71:1-6).

Did you live sexually pure today?
    Yes   *No*

Are you committed to staying sexually pure?
    Yes   *No*

Notes

DAY 9
Reality of Relationships

We want it! We need it! We were made to have it! We'll do just about anything to get it! I'm speaking of relationships: family, friends, boyfriends, girlfriends, husband, wife... We can't live without relationships!

Question 1. What is important to you in a relationship (family, friend, boy/ girlfriend – your choice)?

Question 2. What are some characteristics you desire in your future husband or wife? Have some fun making a list!

Question 3. Do you believe your desires for your mate are really possible for you to enjoy one day?

    A. Yes
    B. No
    C. Don't really know

Is achieving your desires possible? Yes! In fact, God *wants* to grant you what your heart truly desires. He is not in heaven devising ways to hurt you and keep you from happiness. God *wants* to open the floodgates of heaven and pour out His blessing onto you. He *wants* to give you the desires of your heart! He knows your heart better than you do and he is eager to fulfill those desires He's planted there. But first, He *wants* you to delight in Him.

Read His promise in Psalm 37:4, Delight yourself in the Lord and He will give you the desires of your heart.

Question 4. How does this verse make you feel about God's thoughts toward you?

Question 5. Is delighting yourself in the Lord, or enjoying your relationship with Him the most important thing in your life? Would you like it to be? Explain.

On Tuesday, July 24, 2001, in front of several thousand people at a youth conference, I (Nathan) proposed to the love of my life. She was surprised, but said "Yes", (thank God), and we were married the following November. We are so happy and so in love. But let me take you back, back before she was the love of my life. Things weren't always so warm and fuzzy between us. In fact, early in our relationship we struggled to even be friends – definitely no thoughts of marriage! Looking back, we both see this as God's gracious and protective hand at work. Because there were no romantic thoughts and feelings at first, it enabled us to do two things: stay focused on our relationship with Christ, and get to know each other, learning to be friends without the stress of romance. As we both kept our relationship with Christ number one, He grew our friendship to the point of true love. God engineered our relationship the whole way, lining up common interests and life goals, while fulfilling our heart's desires in each other. As we delighted ourselves in Him, He granted us the desires of our hearts! I now love this woman with all my heart and am enjoying everything about our relationship. More than anything, I love the way my wife loves Jesus above everything, including me. Because our first and most important delight was and is our relationship with Jesus, He has granted us the desires of our hearts and beyond!

Question 6. What do you think it means in practical, daily terms to "delight yourself in the Lord"?

Course member Randall, age 18, writes: Delighting in God first shifts my focus off what I want to receive from a relationship with others (guys or girls). It helps me focus on what God wants from my relationship with them, how I can point them to Christ, and encourage them.

Course member Ashlie, age 18, writes: When your first love is God and you want to obey him first, then you learn to see other people as He sees them. That's when you become less selfish in relationships and learn to love people the way God loves them. You will treat them better and in return they will treat you better also.

Time in God's Word and in prayer is definitely the foundation. Just as a relationship with a husband and wife is more than just routinely talking, so is a relationship with the Lord. To delight in someone or something means so much more than simply doing the minimum to please or appreciate them.

Think about how you eat your absolute favorite food. Do you just stick it in your mouth, and gulp it down in one big chunk? That's doubtful if it's your favorite food! Instead, you probably stick it on your fork, eagerly look at what you are about to enjoy, inhale the wonderful smell and then place a good sized portion of it in your mouth, to slowly chew and savor every ounce of taste before you swallow it...then go back for more.

Now, (as you're on your way to the fridge) think about your relationship with Jesus. Is your relationship with Jesus like eating just because you have to or you'll die, or is it more like eating because you really enjoy the feast placed before you?

Psalm 34:8 says, "O taste and see that the Lord is good;..." Have you savored your relationship with Jesus lately? Do you savor Him? Or are you in the habit of simply paying Him "respect" by asking Him to bless your food, your half-hearted commitment to Him, and by going to church once a week with your parents? If these habits are yours, some major changes need to be made. If it is your desire to have good, dynamic, passionate relationships now and in your future, you must decide now to delight yourself in God above all else and seek to know Him and His will every day. Only that will make a difference in your other relationships. God is the creator of relationships. He holds the answers to all your relationship questions. But first, He desires to be the most important relationship you have. If He is that, God promises to give you the desires of your heart, and He always is true to His promises!

Question 7. In the space below write three practical things you are going to do to delight in God above all.

We know that we are to delight in relationships. We are first of all to delight ourselves in the Lord, and secondly we are to delight ourselves in our future mate. But we must understand that the key to delighting in these relationships is to walk in purity. Sin is that horrible stuff that breaks and destroys relationships, and in order to enjoy God and others, purity must be part of our lives. Indeed, while the vast majority of you who are reading these words will get married, it may not be for several years - and God may even have a single life planned for some of you. Either way, it is very, very important to know that God is sufficient, regardless of whether we are married or single, and that a life of purity is still the goal.

Did you know that God made you in order to enjoy you? Did you know that your purpose on this earth is to enjoy the Lord and to make Him known to others? If this is true, and Scripture teaches that it is, then we will never be happy until we are happy in God. We will never be fulfilled until we are worshiping, adoring and rejoicing in God. We all long for a relationship with God, and we are not ever content until we enjoy and delight in Him. And how do we learn to enjoy the Lord? Purity is the answer! How do we discover the enjoyment of Jesus Christ? We commit to, and live out a pure life. This means we reject evil, we turn our backs on things that other teens seem to enjoy, and we purposefully set out to find our happiness in Christ.

We started this day talking about the need we all have for relationships. That need is given to us by God, and it's wonderful, because He wants a relationship with us. However, since the need for relationships is given by God, the way to maintain and enjoy relationships should also be given by God. His design is for relationships to be a pure picture of Him. Purity is the great promoter of relationships, whereas sinful impurity is that which destroys relationships. Purity keeps relationships truthful, open, selfless and loving – all the ingredients to a growing relationship. Impurity breeds deceit, hiding, and selfishness – the means to destroy any relationship.

Question 8. What is the "great promoter" of relationships?

Question 9. What is the destroyer of relationships?

Question 10. Please record your thoughts about purity as the key to good relationships.

17-year-old Julie writes: When I spend time with God, I develop a love relationship with Him. I understand how much He loves me. Therefore, it helps me to pass on this love to others. If I'm delighting in God, then I'm more likely to look out for other's needs more often than my own.

Scripture to Consider

Jesus prayed for us in John 17:20-22: "My prayer is not for them alone. I pray also for those who will believe in me through their message, that all of them may be one, Father, just as you are in me and I am in you. May they also be in us so that the world may believe that you have sent me."

Did you live sexually pure today?
        Yes   *No*

Are you committed to staying sexually pure?
        Yes   *No*

Notes

DAY 10
Reality of Dating

Today's lesson will look at another reality of teen years. The surge of hormones that was discussed on Day 8 is a part of the reality of who you are, and the desire for relationships (Day 9) is also part of who you are. So that naturally leads us to another reality topic—Dating.

It is the fulfillment of Genesis 2:24 that "a man will leave his father and mother and be joined to his wife, and they will become one flesh." The desire for companionship in relationships is also God-created. Therefore, dating in and of itself is not evil or harmful, it's great. It can be fun and useful, but how someone dates can greatly impact and even ruin his or her purity! Therefore, this lesson will address the stumbling blocks to avoid and the stepping-stones to take in order to preserve your purity while you are dating and afterward while married. Remember who you are—heirs of God, a sinner who's been justified, and because of Christ, extremely valuable!

A guy and girl who were going out for the very first time. The guy showed up at her house right on time and was quite the gentleman as he spoke with her father while he was waiting, and then escorted the girl out to the car. He opened the passenger door and helped her into the car before shutting the door and walking around the car to the driver's side.

Well, the girl was so nervous before he arrived at her house she had gotten very bad hiccups. Her sister told her to drink a full glass of coke quickly to relieve the hiccups, which, surprisingly had worked wonderfully. Now, the only trouble was she had so much air built up inside, she felt the uncontrollable need to let out a really big burp. She felt the strong urge as she walked down the stairs to greet her date, and she had been successful at holding it as he helped her into the car. Now, alone in the car for a few seconds, she decided she had to ease her discomfort. She opened her mouth and let out the longest, strongest burp she'd ever heard! As her date opened his door and slid into the car, she smiled at him, relieved he hadn't heard anything and that now she was comfortable and ready to enjoy the evening. He put his keys into the ignition and turning to her said, "I don't know if you've met my brother and his girlfriend. They will be double-dating with us tonight." As he said this, he pointed over his shoulder to the couple sitting, smirking, in the back seat.

Dating can be a fun, exciting, stressful, or even an embarrassing time! Involving others you respect and trust in your dating experience – both to guide you and laugh with you – is vitally important. Some people believe that courtship (parentally supervised dating for the purpose of marriage) is better suited to promoting purity in the Christian life than just "dating" without much involvement by the parents. Teens, please realize the great gift you have in your parents! Communicate openly with them about your desires and relationships. Utilize them if they want to be involved in your life as you choose with whom you will spend time, who you will date or court, and who you will marry! If your parents are godly, they can help you greatly in this area, and you need to pursue and follow their wisdom, guidance and authority. They are a gift from God to you in this area of dating. If your parents are not available to help you, seek other strong, godly Christians who will help you choose wisely whom you will date and who will hold you accountable to purity as you date.

Question 1. Let's first consider the purpose of dating. In the space below, describe what you believe to be the purpose of dating.

>**17-year-old Julie writes:** I date to get to know someone better. I want to have a good time on my dates, but if it's uncomfortable because the guy seems to want something else, then I know not to date him anymore.

>**18-year-old Randall writes:** Right now I date because I like a girl. But I also want to know what some of the things are that will be a part of having a relationship with someone. What will she expect of me? What are the best types of dates? I won't even consider dating a non-Christian girl. It would compromise who I am, and my leadership in my youth group. But I feel that when I choose someone to date, I must choose a Christian girl who is going in the same direction I am.

In our society the goal of dating has become skewed. In light of Genesis 2:24, an important goal of dating should be to find the one that God has designed for you, and will complete you. This will be the one for whom you will want to leave your parents to become one flesh under the covenant of marriage. Whether you use the term dating or courting, it's important for you to seek to learn who you are and who God has created you to need in order to be complete. To be complete, you need more than a good-looking person. God's reality is: to be complete, you need to pursue Jesus Christ above everything. He will fill you and complete you like nothing else, and then dating takes on a new perspective.

Dating/courtship should be fun, and a profitable time for learning who you are through the similarities and differences in the people you date. Often though, dating is not motivated by learning about yourself and the other person. Instead it is driven by lust and the immediate satisfaction of desires or the need to never be alone. This is where courting may be a better alternative as it assists in maintaining purity. It's true that any relationship based on lust and selfishness is destined for failure because it is based on an illusion, not the reality of who we are and should be.

> **Course member Lindsey writes:** Before I was saved I was boy crazy. I was insecure in myself and would pounce on any guy who was the least bit interested in me - even if I didn't really like them. I was so into guys and myself that I didn't care who I hurt or what I did to get a guy. I went from guy to guy. Even in the church when I first started going, I must have dated at least half of the guys in the youth group. Then one day it dawned on me. Without God and with me still living in my sin, I was on my way to hell. I decided then and there to once and for all give my life completely to the Lord. At first, I still fell in regards to guys, but now I haven't dated anyone in over a year and I'm being freed from self-gratification as well as lusting after guys and constantly wanting a boyfriend to fill my every need. God is good.

Decide now not to let your dating life become a world of illusion. If you are only dating now to satisfy your immediate desires and you are more focused on receiving than giving, you are living in a world of illusion and your relationship is destined to fail. If you allow illusion now, then you will allow it in marriage. Successful, real relationships later are based on **real, pure** relationships now.

Whether you court or date, keep your communication with your parents open about it! **Guys,** if you meet a girl who loves God and is intriguing, don't be too afraid or lazy to ask to spend some time getting to know her. Show her how a strong godly man lives and has a blast enjoying God and life! Show her God in you. Show her the reality of a pure man loving God first and enjoying life! She probably isn't used to seeing that and doesn't quite know what it looks like. But what a great high standard you'd set for her!

Ladies, do you know that dating isn't the measure for how important or how beautiful you are? It's true. So whether you single-date, group date or just hang with friends, learn who you are and what kind of godly character traits you're looking for in a man! Have fun. Be observant. Be wise. Be aware. Be strong. Guard your heart. Be true to the real you, created by God. **Don't ever sacrifice the reality of purity for an illusion of acceptance or reassurance**. Dating cannot fulfill you – only God can. You will date better and enjoy relationships better when you know that and can live in that mindset.

Course member Katie writes: I had the typical Jr. High days – I had to like someone at all times, because everybody did! I pursued guys (which wasn't my job) and if he was cute and nice, I liked him! The day after I stopped liking one guy, the next guy was in my thoughts. I didn't make time for God with all the guys in my head! But then, I decided to give up my life to God and NOT search for guys. If God wanted me to have a boyfriend it would happen, but I wasn't going to go looking for one. So I prayed that if I am supposed to be dating, God would give me some indication. Two months later my current boyfriend was placed right in front of me when I met him at youth group, and my purity has been totally blossoming ever since. When we first met, I thought he was sooo cute, and he was a very deep Christian. We started doing stuff together just as friends and I kept praying that if this is the one for me to date, let me know! The indicators just flowed on. We started going out 5 months ago and we talk about purity all the time. It's amazing how much you can learn in such a short time. God showed me that to be pure inside and out, I have to WANT it, - pursue it, practice it and learn more of it. I am still learning too!

Question 2. Write some qualities of a person you would like to marry someday:

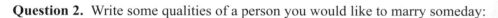

Elizabeth Elliot says, "The Lord taught me that preparing for marriage is not so much a matter of finding the right person as it is becoming the right person. So I began to concentrate on my relationship with Christ." [11]

Question 3. Are you pursuing the qualities you listed above in your own life? (Remember that a person with these qualities will only be drawn to the same qualities)

Dating is a definite time to be pursuing what you want/need in a marriage partner. It doesn't always have to be serious conversations about five goals for the future, or your "life's mission statement". But dating is definitely beneficial in making

you become the kind of person you need to be and in learning the kind of person with whom you need to be yoked for the rest of your life. Considering your future, life commitment, and the character qualities involved in that should always be in your mind when you're dating. Don't ignore the reality that what you do and whom you date has definite effects in the future. Of course you're not ready to be married at 16 or maybe even 22, but know that you can't date without thinking of what your future will hold if you were to marry this person (or someone with these qualities). With each date, you are either moving toward or away from the future life of which you dream and the one God has designed for you. What direction are you moving in your dating life?
Read these verses and comment on your thoughts below:

Do not be yoked together with unbelievers. For what do righteousness and wickedness have in common? Or what fellowship can light have with darkness? What harmony is there between Christ and Belial? (Satan). What does a believer have in common with an unbeliever? What agreement is there between the temple of God and idols? For we are the temple of the living God. As God said: "I will live with them and walk among them, and I will be their God, and they will be my people. Therefore come out from them and be separate," says the Lord. "Touch no unclean thing and I will receive you" (2 Corinthians 6:14-17, explanation added).

Question 4. In the above verses, what instruction does the author, Paul, give?

Question 5. We also see a promise and a condition in the above verses. What does God promise us, and what must we do to attain the promise?

Question 6. In your own words, apply this Scripture to what has been discussed so far about dating, and getting to know other people.

16-year-old Crystal writes: You must discern in your spirit the character of the people you are around; some may profess to be a Christian but could just be saying that..... You will know them by their fruit. Don't date or marry unbelievers, it's like good and evil…they are still in the kingdom of darkness…but you have been brought into the kingdom of light, the kingdom of God. When you date or marry an unbeliever and become unequally yoked it's like dating the enemy. And not only that but they can drag you down and pull you away from God; a relationship with them can take you far away from Him (God).

We hope that you can see the significance in all this. In the above Scripture, Paul warns believers not to become linked – or yoked – with unbelievers. Why? Because when we do we risk being linked with wickedness and darkness and as a result can distance ourselves from God. Therefore it is extremely important to know the person you are with. Reality - are they drawing you to God and toward reality, or away from God to illusion? You will always be moving one way or the other. No one is ever static.

King Solomon loved many foreign women, besides Pharaoh's daughter— Moabites, Ammonites, Edomites, Sidonians, and Hittites. They were from the nations about which the Lord had told the Israelites, "You must not intermarry with them, because they will surely turn your hearts after their gods." Nevertheless, Solomon held fast to them in love. He had seven hundred wives of royal birth and three hundred concubines, and his wives led him astray. As Solomon grew old, his wives turned his heart after other gods, and his heart was not fully devoted to the Lord his God, as the heart of David his father had been. He followed Ashtoreth the goddess of the Sidonians, and Molech the detestable god of the Ammonites. So Solomon did evil in the eyes of the Lord; he did not follow the Lord completely, as David his father had done (1 Kings 11:1-6).

Question 7. In the verse above, the Lord gave the children of Israel the commandment not to intermarry with foreign nations. Why?
   A. Family get-togethers would be brutal
   B. They would turn away the Israelites'
       hearts toward their other gods
   C. Filing taxes would be very difficult

Question 8. According to the verses, was King Solomon strong enough to remain loyal to God in spite of all these wives who did not love God?

Even mighty King Solomon, when he ruled over the kingdom of Israel at its greatest with God-given wisdom, could not keep himself from destruction. King Solomon allowed himself to become entangled with wives who did not follow and believe in God. His heart and loyalty became divided, and the end result was God's anger falling upon him and having the kingdom pulled away from him. Please, do not try this at home! Seek a mate who knows and loves God, so that your heart can be encouraged toward the same, rather than turned away from Him.

Through this course you have been making choices to live a life of purity. It is vital to know that whomever you date now or in the future respects and shares your pursuit of purity. They need to share the same faith and beliefs in God and Jesus that you do. Many have gone into relationships thinking they can change the other person. Although this is a nice thought, often what happens is that they change you, and you end up sacrificing your own beliefs and morals. It will be extremely difficult, if not impossible, for only one person in a dating relationship to be committed to purity and have it succeed. Think through that.

"One graduate of an Ivy League college told me that only one man had asked her out a second time. The others, learning that she would not go to bed, never called her again. The one who did call thought perhaps she was just being coy. He thought that on the second date she might be persuaded."[12] This wise woman stood her ground even though she lost dates.

Someone wrote to an advice columnist, "I get so tired of women always wanting to get serious. I enjoy women and like to date, but all I want is a little diversion and a few laughs." The columnist's advice to the writer: "Then take a hyena to lunch!"[13]

Question 9. Have your views and attitudes toward dating changed after taking this lesson? How so?

Question 10. If you are dating a person who does not wish to pursue purity and reality of who you each are before God, what will you do?

Question 11. Please record any other comments or thoughts you may have on this lesson.

Scripture to Consider

Daughters of Jerusalem, I charge you: Do not arouse or awaken love until it so desires. Place me like a seal over your heart, like a seal on your arm; for love is as strong as death, its jealousy unyielding as the grave. It burns like blazing fire, like a mighty flame. Many waters cannot quench love; rivers cannot wash it away. If one were to give all the wealth of his house for love, it would be utterly scorned (Song of Solomon 8: 4,6,7).

Did you live sexually pure today?
      Yes   *No*

Are you committed to staying sexually pure?
      Yes   *No*

DAY 11
Love

This is a fun lesson today. We get to talk about a topic that makes your skin tingle and your ears perk up just by saying the word. You've all experienced it in some sense and form. You've all felt it in different ways and you've all seen it happen in different ways. This topic can either make you gag or make you make you giggle, depending on who you're sitting next to in a movie. It's something that more songs have been written about than any other topic. And there are even more stories written about it. The topic today is love. How do you picture love?

An old couple sat down at a table in a restaurant. The waitress came up and asked them if she could get them anything. "Yes," said the old man," Could you please bring us a glass of water?" "Would you each like a glass of water?" the waitress asked. "Oh, no thank you", smiled the lovely old woman. "We'll share it. We share everything."

A few minutes later the waitress appeared again and asked if there was anything else she could get for them. "Would you please bring us a piece of pie and two plates?" grinned the old man. "You don't each want a piece of pie?" the waitress asked. "Oh no, one piece will do just fine. We'll share it. We share everything,"

A short time later the waitress came to the table again and saw the old man enjoying his portion of the pie while his wife sat with her hands folded on her lap and her portion untouched.
"Is everything O.K.?" she asked the woman. "I see you haven't touched your piece of the pie yet." "Yes, everything is fine, Honey, "she smiled." I'm just waiting for my turn with the teeth."

Okay, so maybe that's not the type of "love" you picture yourself enjoying someday! No matter, let's talk about love and the truth behind it. Today we discuss love... not the "feeling" of love, or the "confusion" of love, but the true reality of love. We will learn what love is, what it looks like, its enemy and how to pursue it correctly. Enjoy this topic today! For you were created out of love, and created to love.

Question 1. Before we go any further, write your own definition of love. Put into words how you would describe love...

What is Love?

This is Webster's Dictionary definition of "love":
1. a deep and tender feeling of fondness and devotion;
2. a strong liking;
3. a sweetheart;
4. in tennis, a score of zero.

Knowing the ever-changing world in which we live, none of those definitions sound like something on which to base a life. What happens when those "tender feelings of fondness" or "strong likings" change? By the definitions above, love is subject to change at any time. So is there a more concrete definition of love? Yes! In 1 John 4:16, the Bible gives this definition of love, it says: *"...God is love."* That definition is not based on changing feelings or a changing world. That definition is based on an unchanging God who is the author and creator of love. He is the definition of love, therefore we will look to Him and His Words to us in order to learn more about love.

The Look of Love

Read these verses about love and answer the question below.

Love is patient, love is kind. It does not envy, it does not boast, it is not proud. It is not rude, it is not self seeking, it is not easily angered, it keeps no record of wrongs. Love does not delight in evil but rejoices with the truth. It always protects, always trusts, always hopes, always perseveres. Love never fails (1 Corinthians 13:4-8).

Question 2. From the verses above, list all the things that the Bible says love is:

From the list above, we get a clear picture of the way God created love to look among us. Love looks unselfish, pure, hopeful, persevering. Love is not only about happy feelings and just finding someone to marry. It is a way of life. Probably you have experienced some clear pictures of that kind of love written about in 1 Corinthians. Think of all the places and ways you've felt and seen glimpses of that kind of "love". Maybe your parents have given you a good picture of it. Or maybe you've experienced portions of it from your friends, from your brother or sister, from a boyfriend or girlfriend; or maybe even from a coach or teacher or pastor.

All those experiences and feelings are a very real part of love. Please be careful not to assume you already know what love is because you've had a boyfriend or girlfriend. You must understand the "fullness" of love, or the "completeness" of love in order to understand true love. Yes, you can experience loving feelings as a young person, and even live and act out of love, but a "full" or "complete" love is designed to be experienced between a husband and wife in a marriage that has Jesus Christ at the center. Part of being "heirs of God" is the ability to fully enjoy and desire His true blessings, despite whatever else is offered to you in this world. One of those blessings God has for you is the enjoyment of <u>real</u> love; not a fake version of love, but real, complete love. Using the verses above from 1 Corinthians 13, we have a great picture of what real love looks and acts like.

The Enemy of Love

Because God is love and Satan hates God, He tries to tempt us with imitations of love. He seeks to get us to settle for his incomplete, selfish version of "love". We call it lust. The enemy of love is lust. They are opposites. At the core of love is unselfishness, serving, and sacrificing. But lust has at its core, selfishness, pride and illusion. Lust is Satan's perverted, twisted, never-satisfying substitute for real love. Lust is a selfish and unbridled sexual urge that, if followed, always ends in guilt, pain and destruction. Lust and infatuation can go hand in hand. Infatuation is incomplete love. Infatuation is largely based on physical attraction and the image and perceptions we have of the other person, not <u>who</u> the person really is, created by God. True love cannot abide where lust resides, just as a room cannot be both light and dark at the same time. Let's look at how love and lust compare.

Question 3. Read those above verses from I Corinthians 13 again. For each trait of love below, think of an opposite trait that describes lust:

If love is patient, then lust is <u>hurried and impatient</u>.

If love is kind, then lust is <u>rude or uncaring.</u>

If love is humble, then lust is _____

If love is selfless, then lust is _____

If love trusts, then lust _____

If love is slow to anger, then lust is _____

If love forgives, then lust _____

If love protects, then lust _____

If love perseveres in the face of difficulties, then lust _____

If love continues until the end, then lust _____

If love gives freedom, then lust _____

If love encourages purity, then lust _____

Only true, complete love anchored in the Person of Jesus Christ can fulfill you and God's design for you. Lust will only hurt you and those for whom you care.

The following testimony is from Jen: I once dated this guy who was the "perfect" guy. He was gorgeous, athletic, fun and he was highly attracted to me. Everyone else thought he was a "player", but I knew Shawn really liked me for who I was. He'd tell me I was beautiful all the time and wasn't afraid to put his arm around me in public. What a mature guy I thought he was. He used to also tell me constantly what a gorgeous body I had. He would protect me from other guys who wanted to compliment me or try to ask me out. I knew Shawn loved me. The way he kissed me and hugged me told me everything he was feeling. But soon, he started wanting to go further and further. He wanted to see and touch parts of me that were reserved for my husband someday.

Rumors eventually reached me that he was telling stories in the locker room about our open sexual relationship—which was a lie. I tried to talk to him about it, but he just told me I didn't understand the way guys exaggerate and that I should trust him because we loved each other. I asked him how he knows he loves me, and once again he told me that I was beautiful and the only one who ever made him feel so special. Again, I believed him. It wasn't until later that year, when things between us had cooled down, that I saw him for what he really was. A new girl came to school. Shawn was the first to welcome her and "show her around". One day at lunch I overheard the new girl telling some other girls how Shawn had really made her feel special and beautiful and that the way he kissed her told her everything she wondered about how he felt toward her. I was so hurt and so mad. Shawn's attraction to me was not love; it was the furthest thing from it. Pure lust is what he had for me, and that faded and found a new object to desire way too fast. That's not the kind of relationship I want to have ever again.

How to Know Love

This is how we know what love is: Jesus Christ laid down his life for us. And we ought to lay down our lives for our brothers (1 John 3:16).

Love gives of itself for the benefit of another. True love is most clearly exhibited as Jesus Christ laid down His life for us. Scriptures teach us that He gave up heaven and the glory that was His from all eternity, to come to earth as a Man, become a servant to those He had created, and then because of His love for us, while we were still sinners, Christ died for us. (Romans 5:8) Because of God's love for us, He sent His one and only Son that whoever believes in Him, will not perish, but will have eternal life. (John 3:16) He died in our place to pay for our sins. His love for sinners like us drove Him to the cross, where He suffered for us, and then died for us. This is real love. Compared to this real love and the eternal relationship we can have with God because of this sacrificial love, lust has nothing to offer.

Be careful not to allow yourself to camp in enemy territory. Living with lust is like living with the enemy. It is risky, dangerous and unwise. Following anything the enemy has to offer will not just hurt you, it will eventually destroy you. And of course, that is the plan of the Evil One – your destruction. Whereas, Jesus Christ came that you may have life, and have it to the fullest. (John 10:10).

Question 4. Please take a moment and describe how Jesus' dying on the cross reveals what true love is.

It is the most amazing thing when someone of the opposite sex says, "I love you." Suddenly you feel yourself energized with emotion, giddy with excitement, and consumed with thoughts about them. But how do you know if you are being truly loved by the one who says those three magical words? Why not examine those words in the light of what the Bible says true love is? Why not compare it to the greatest exhibition of love there ever has been, which was Jesus Christ laying down His life for us? Is the one who says "I love you" giving up his/her desires, wishes and wants, and forgoing personal pleasure, in consideration of you? Are they sacrificing their own desires for sexual pleasure in order to help you stay pure?

Love is a decision. It is a choice to pursue the best in the other person and to help him or her be a success in God's eyes. Yes, there can definitely be romantic feelings in that kind of "decisive" love. But true love is not based only on romantic feelings that come and go. It is a decision that transcends feelings. It is a choice. Included in the choice to love someone is the choice to be pure and help them be pure as well. You cannot separate love from purity. You will know that the one saying, "I love you" truly loves you if he wants to see you successful in God's eyes, and is willing to sacrifice his own pleasure for purity in both of you.

Read through the following scenarios, and place an "X" in the proper place that shows whether there is real love happening here, or whether it is merely lust.

1. You are a high school girl, and a boy you have really gotten to like asks you to the prom. When you tell him that your father has insisted on driving you and the boy to the prom and back, the boy responds, "Oh brother, why can't we have any time alone? Prom night is the time to really get to know each other, if you know what I mean."

      Possible love _____   Lust _____

2. You are a 17 year-old guy who is committed to purity, which, for you, means not allowing yourself to be alone with any girl where there would be occasion for temptation and possible sin. When you explain this to a girl who has caught your eyes, she replies, "That makes me very happy to hear. I, too, am willing to do whatever it takes to stay pure."

      Possible love _____   Lust _____

3. As a guy you are taking a night class, and have become friends with a pretty girl who sits next to you. One night she is dressed in clothing that is quite revealing, and she passes you a note that says, "Meet me at my car after class. My parents aren't home, so let's have some fun."

      Possible love _____   Lust _____

4. You are a 16-year-old girl who longs to enjoy Christ and knows that purity is a requirement for it. There is an older boy with whom you have fallen in love. He is well-respected as a Christian and is going away to seminary in the fall. He has told you "I love you" and you feel as though he means it, as there is much emotion in his voice when he says it. He has asked you if you and he can be alone one night before he leaves, as he wants to make you a promise and really show you how much he loves you.

      Possible love _____   Lust _____

5. You always go to church on Wed. night and you like having fun there with your friends. Recently someone you really like has been wanting to hang out

with you more. You like being with that person, so you invite them to church with you, but they laugh and tell you they won't go someplace with so many hypocrites and instead invite you to a party so you can really have a good time.

Possible love _____   Lust _____

How to Pursue Love

There are many places to get pictures of love as we described earlier: parents, friends, siblings, girlfriends or boyfriends, a coach, teacher or pastor. Although those do not give us the fullness or completeness of love, all those experiences and feelings are a very real part of understanding love. They definitely show us that we all have a God-given desire to know and experience love. But as we also mentioned earlier, they are small pieces of the great love we all desire. Don't settle for only a small piece or picture of love; pursue the full feast of love!

"How do I pursue love?" you ask. It is not found in adding phone numbers to your cell phone speed dial. No, girls, you don't need to follow guys to their locker and call them on the telephone every night. (In fact, that is a major turn off to guys!) And guys, you don't need to beat up every guy that looks twice at the girl you like or send an "innocent party" over to talk to her. No, those kinds of pursuits last no longer than the TV show that encourages it. But there is a way to pursue lasting love. Here is the key: **The complete depth of love can only be experienced through a growing relationship with Jesus Christ!** Since God is love (1 John 4:16) and Jesus is God (John 10:30), the best way to know and experience love is through Jesus Christ. All your hopes and dreams lie in Him! Don't be afraid to pursue Him as your heart craves love. He will care for your heart in ways no other person ever can. In so pursuing Him, he will love you, and give you peace, strength and unbelievable insight for the ways you can also love other people. If He has plans to give you a spouse someday, he will prepare your heart to love your spouse by first teaching you how to love Him. When you pursue Jesus Christ above all, you will never be disappointed. You will truly know Love.

Question 5. How has this lesson shaped your views on what love is, what it isn't and how to tell the difference?

Question 6. Do you feel more able to know when you love someone, or when someone else loves you? Are there things in your relationships that are not characterized by this complete, selfless, committed love that may need to be radically amputated? (More on Radical Amputation on Day 17.)

Question 7. What are your thoughts about love right now?

Scripture to Consider

This is how we know what love is: Jesus Christ laid down his life for us. And we ought to lay down our lives for our brothers. If anyone has material possessions and sees his brother in need but has no pity on him, how can the love of God be in him? Dear children, let us not love with words or tongue but with actions and in truth (1 John 3:16-18).

Did you live sexually pure today?
        Yes   *No*

Are you committed to staying sexually pure?
        Yes   *No*

DAY 12
'Til Death Do You Part

On November 24, 2001, before hundreds of people and before God, I (Jena) looked into Nathan's eyes and answered the question, "Do you promise to love, honor and cherish this man, 'till death do you part?" Before all those people and God, my answer was a whole-hearted "Yes". But what does that mean? To what did I commit? Was I just agreeing to a good "deal," or simply making a contract to live together? Was I taking the best offer I'd received and just trying to make the most of it? No way! On November 24, Nathan and I made a <u>commitment</u> before God, to each other, for life. We said we would be committed until death parted us. So what does that mean?

Question 1. What's your definition of commitment? How/where have you seen commitment in action?

Commitment is an agreement or a pledge to do something. Commitment is based more on your personal integrity and word than the surrounding circumstances. In Dr. H. Norman Wright's video for marriage counseling, he says that a commitment is different from a contract because a commitment cannot be voided if one party does not hold up their side of the agreement. In a contract, if one side breaks it, the whole contract is void. A commitment however, means we promise to uphold **our** side to love, honor, and cherish each other before God, no matter what happens. A commitment in marriage is for life. When this commitment is made in purity, there is great safety, security and freedom to be totally unified with each other physically, emotionally and spiritually.

Course member Matt writes: Well, as I've worked through this course I had my doubts whether or not it would work for me. I was always on the verge of giving up on the whole purity thing. I was willing to try anything. My will failed, my prayers didn't help me because there was still doubt in my heart. I saw others enjoying purity and I always thought it was some act that they put on to hide the real sin inside. So I enrolled in this course one day when my mentor recommended it to me. I was skeptical and had fallen a few times during my 30 days. But you know what? Jesus didn't give up, even when I had. He still kept pressing me and leading me and strengthening me.

But what might hinder us from experiencing this great safety, security and freedom with each other? What might keep a person from upholding their commitment daily? Impurity. Impurity is a destroyer of relationships. It is a temporary substitute for long-lasting enjoyment. Before we (Nathan and Jena) were married, purity was a daily battle we had to fight. Even now, purity is still something we must both pursue in order to have an enjoyable, intimate, God-pleasing relationship in marriage. **Purity means living right in the God-given context you are in every day!** Purity as a teen means remaining free from sex outside marriage and other intimate activities that may lead to improper sexual desires. Purity in marriage involves faithfulness to your partner, communication, truthfulness, and a single focus. So understand that there is **always** a necessity for purity in your life! If you want a great marriage, help it now by learning how to make a commitment to purity, and how to receive God's grace to keep that commitment for life!

Question 2. Explain in your own words how learning to live in purity now will affect your future.

God promises great reward and blessing when we abide by His Words and live according to His standards. Let me tell you, purity is a difficult struggle. We are all in it together! But I am so thankful for the riches and intimacy of a marriage relationship that is totally based on, and blessed by God. That's purity! And that's the driving force that helped us fight for purity before our wedding and especially now after we're married. Satan will seek to create all kinds of illusions and distract us from what is right and pure. So, learn purity and what it means to be committed to purity now! It will help you as you enjoy deeper relationships now and in the days to come.

Today we are talking about commitment—especially commitment in marriage and commitment in purity. A commitment is a serious thing. When you have bacon and eggs for breakfast you know that a chicken was involved. But the pig was committed. We want to help you learn how to commit to purity now so that your future commitment to marriage can also be affected by your commitment to purity. Decide in your heart right now before the Lord that, not only will you remain pure before marriage, but you will also be pure in marriage and remain married for life. This whole course is aimed at purity and your commitment to it, but it's also important for you to have a clear view of the commitment involved in marriage so you can understand why purity **right now** is such a necessity in preparing for a committed, pure marriage.

Question 3. Marriage is a gift from God. We should prepare for it and protect it. What are your thoughts in regards to your purity right now?

Commitment in our lives goes beyond just agreeing with an idea. Commitment is a personal promise to stick with something, no matter what circumstances may come. There are many ways you can be committed in relationships even now. Think of your friendships. Are there times when it would be easier to just walk away from a friend when the friendship is tough? Or do you know what it feels like to defend a friend or be loyal to someone you love because you have a commitment to them that's bigger than the immediate circumstance? We can see a great picture of commitment even in nature. "Canadian geese (and swans) mate for life. Mated pairs not only raise and protect their young together, but also look out for one another over the course of their lives. One mate will stay by the other's side if injured or dying, even if the rest of the flock is moving on. They are extremely devoted to one another." (www.canadageese.org)
In order for us to get a right picture of what commitment looks like in relationships, we have to look at Jesus. He was committed to loving us and doing what his Heavenly Father wanted no matter what happened to him!

Later, knowing that all was now completed, and so that the Scripture would be fulfilled, Jesus said, 'I am thirsty.' A jar of wine vinegar was there, so they soaked a sponge in it, put the sponge on a stalk of the hyssop plant, and lifted it to Jesus' lips. When he had received the drink, Jesus said, 'It is finished.' With that, he bowed his head and gave up his spirit (John 19:28-30).

Jesus said, "Father, forgive them for they do not know what they are doing" (Luke 23:34).

What a picture of commitment Jesus gives us! Even when people were brutally killing him, He was committed to completing His Father's plan. Jesus was committed to those for whom He was dying and even prayed that God would forgive them! Jesus is a great picture of commitment in relationships and life. Purity was a theme in Jesus' life. He is our example of a perfect, pure human. We have so much to learn from Him! Even through struggle, pain and loneliness He remained committed to God, purity, and us, His bride!

Question 4. What are some things to which you are committed? Not just good ideas, but to what or whom are you totally committed right now?

Question 5. Will you decide now that if you get married in the future, you will commit your life to your partner and never break that commitment? Will you decide that now and pray for the strength to stick to it?

Learn from Jesus' style of commitment. Learn how to be a committed person, by seeing how Jesus is a Friend who sticks closer than a brother. Learn to commit to purity now and in your future relationships. Commitment is not something of which to be afraid, but something to pursue with the strength and guidance of Jesus' example. We are all committed to something. To what are you committed? If it is yourself, your own pleasure, your own personal benefit no matter the cost, you will suffer greatly in life and relationships. If you are committed to Jesus Christ, the pure life and relationships that He models for us, you will be content and blessed beyond your imagination! It is only then that you can truly say to someone, "till death do us part", and have the hope and confidence that Jesus wants that as much as you do and he will help you make that reality!

Scripture to Consider

"A man of many companions may come to ruin, but there is a Friend who sticks closer than a brother" (Proverbs18:24).

Did you live sexually pure today?
        Yes   No

Are you committed to staying sexually pure?
        Yes   No

74

DAY 13
Be Complete

Our son loves Sesame Street. Today the puppets were singing a song describing life without noses, and how funny and difficult that would be! By the end of the song, each puppet had successfully attached a perfect nose to their face and they were all happy again.

Well, that is not the kind of "completeness" we are going to talk about today. We are talking about being "completed" through God's gift of marriage and sex. God's design for humans was to be not alone. Instead, he made a way to make us more complete by giving us marriage, and even more specifically, sex.

God created sex. God created us to have sex. That is not our only, most important purpose or we'd be no different from animals. God gave us sex as a gift to enjoy with the spouse to whom we are committed for life. But there are other purposes for sex.

So God created man in his own image, in the image of God he created him; male and female he created them. God blessed them, and God said to them, "Be fruitful, and increase in number; fill the earth, and subdue it" (Genesis 1:27, 28).

One of the purposes of sex according to God is to increase mankind, fill the earth and subdue it. It accomplishes a tremendous purpose – reproducing human life. God is wise in creating a practical way to accomplish a task that needed to be done – filling the earth. He told Noah and his family the same thing after the Great Flood. "Then God blessed Noah and his sons, saying to them, 'Be fruitful, and increase in number and fill the earth.'" (Genesis 9:1) That's one purpose for sex – to produce offspring.

Now here's another purpose for sex:
The LORD God said, "It is not good for the man to be alone. I will make a helper suitable for him.... For this reason a man will leave his father and mother and be united to his wife, and they will become one flesh" (Genesis 2:18, 24).

Another purpose for sex is completion. It is God's idea that people should not be alone. It is God's idea for a man and woman to become one flesh not only in a physical way, but also in a spiritual, emotional and mental way.

Sex is best with the person God has designed to complete us in marriage. Otherwise, there is always something lacking in sex and always something that hinders us from enjoying it to its fullest. Why settle for a cheap substitute of an amazing thing? Let's look further at God's idea of completion for a man and woman:

Now the LORD God had formed out of the ground all the beasts of the field and all the birds of the air. He brought them to the man to see what he would name them; and whatever the man called each living creature, that was its name. So the man gave names to all the livestock, the birds of the air and all the beasts of the field. But for Adam no suitable helper was found. So the LORD God caused the man to fall into a deep sleep; and while he was sleeping, he took one of the man's ribs and closed up the place with flesh. Then the LORD God made a woman from the rib he had taken out of the man, and he brought her to the man. The man said, "This is now bone of my bones and flesh of my flesh; she shall be called 'woman,' for she was taken out of man." For this reason a man will leave his father and mother and be united to his wife, and they will become one flesh. The man and his wife were both naked, and they felt no shame (Genesis 2:19-25).

Question 1. According to the verses above, what did God say was not good?
   A. The water was too wet
   B. The giraffe's neck was too long
   C. The man was alone
   D. The sky was the wrong shade of blue

Question 2. From the verses above, what did God do at first to help Adam see his need for a mate?

Question 3. According to the above verses, was a suitable helper found by Adam?
          Yes   No

Question 4. In these verses we also see God's ultimate solution to this problem. Write the solution out here...

God recognized that man – Adam – was alone and was in need of a helper. God called together all the animals before Adam and gave him the task of naming each one. Yet out of all the animals there was not one suitable enough to be a helpmate to Adam. There was no creature with whom Adam could communicate, share thoughts, or be intimate. Therefore, God put Adam into a deep sleep and from his rib formed the helper Adam sought – woman.

Adam stated, "This is now bone of my bones and flesh of my flesh" (Genesis 2:23). This, then, is completeness, designed and created by God.

Sex is the bridge and the bond that binds a man and a woman together into one flesh. There is no other act that man can perform that so deeply touches our inner selves and opens us up to the other person. This intimacy is why God has placed specific requirements around sex.

God has created mankind with a need for intimacy, oneness and completion. Possibly right now, or for sure as you get older, you will no doubt experience what is called "burning" in 1 Corinthians 7. This "burning" is an intense desire to be one flesh with another, and it is not bad or sinful in itself. It is God's way of telling you that you are in need of a spouse. (Now, some people are given the gift of singleness. This is a good gift, because it allows the one who has it to focus on God alone.)

This "burning" or intense desire can lead to sin, if we do not recognize God's purpose in it all. Some teens feel that strong desire and allow it to control them, leading to all kinds of sexual impurity.

> **Course member Gordon writes:** I accepted Christ's free gift of salvation and forgiveness. My relationship grew with him, but hit a snag when I continued to view porn. I also had gotten my girlfriend into doing anything sexually possible except having intercourse…

> **Course member Christina writes:** My life revolved around sex and alcohol. I became very miserable…. I began searching for God and followed him for a while, until I met a guy I shouldn't have, who attracted me to him. It wasn't long until we were together. Out of shame I left town and stayed with some people from another church…

Those intense desires that are wrongly used always bring guilt and shame, and even allowing those desires to run wild will not stop the burning. God has designed the burning desire to only to be "quenched" as you experience "one flesh" with your spouse in marriage. If the burning is intense, then pursue God even more intensely! Pursue God and purity according to the intensity of your burning! This is God's prescription! Pour your energy into pursuing God with all your heart, mind and strength! "Blessed are those who obey his statutes and seek him with all their heart" (Psalm 119:2).

Some people have the gift of singleness, but most people are designed for marriage, and the intimacy and union that come from it. In fact, most people, even Christians who are walking with God, truly feel as though something is missing in their lives while they are single.   Be careful not to try to fill that hole with something temporary. God has designed you so that only He and the marriage partner He has created for you someday can adequately fill that missing part of you. Let Christ complete you; let Him bring your missing part to you. For now, as you wait for that, seek your completion in Christ. No human will ever complete us the way Jesus Christ can. Being fully completed in Christ is something we will need our entire life.

Next, please read the following passage of Scripture and make comments below:

In this same way, husbands ought to love their wives as their own bodies. He who loves his wife loves himself. After all, no one ever hated his own body, but he feeds and cares for it, just as Christ does the church - for we are members of his body. "For this reason a man will leave his father and mother and be united to his wife, and the two will become one flesh." This is a profound mystery - but I am talking about Christ and the church. However, each one of you also must love his wife as he loves himself, and the wife must respect her husband. (Ephesians 5:28-33).

Question 5. According to the verse above, of what is this "one flesh" a picture?
   A. Siamese twins
   B. Christ and the Church
   C. Adam and Eve

When two people become one, they are picturing the union and intimacy that Jesus Christ has with the church. If we are Christians, He lives in us and we live in Him and we are in an unbreakable union. When man and wife become "one flesh" they are making a picture of the love Jesus has for His bride, the church, and of her submission to Him. This is why the "one flesh" union is sacred and holy, and should not be entered into apart from marriage.

Question 6. Describe in your own words what you believe it means to be "one flesh." What does being "completed" look like?

Remember that being "one flesh" and experiencing "completion" with someone is part of the riches to which you can look forward in marriage. God promises the wait will be worth it and God has never disappointed anyone who truly trusts Him. God's design for completion and one flesh in marriage is reality - a great reality! So don't allow Satan to tempt you to sacrifice a great thing that is to come for a temporary illusion now.

Course member Nate writes: There were many years that I wondered if God would ever "complete" me. Two years ago He brought a woman into my life, a miracle that cannot be rivaled. However, as I look back, I see how God transformed me and prepared me to complete her as well.

Scripture to Consider

Blessed are those who obey his statutes and seek him with all their heart (Psalm 119:2).

Did you live sexually pure today?
        Yes   *No*

Are you committed to staying sexually pure?
        Yes   *No*

Notes

DAY 14
Do I Know You?

The following is a true story:

Kim and Krickitt Carpenter were married and loving life together. They had dated for a while and were married with many family and friends around to celebrate with them. About two months after they were married, as they were driving home for Thanksgiving with family, they were in a terrible car accident in which a semi smashed their vehicle. Krickitt suffered a massive head injury and was near death. They rushed her to the hospital and told the family to be prepared for the worst. After weeks in a coma, Krickitt finally awoke, but her memory had been erased. She did not know her husband. She had no memory of ever meeting him, dating or marrying him. Her husband was devastated. To Krickitt, her husband was a stranger. Kim sought God and pleaded for his wife back. Since her memory was not coming back, he felt strengthened by God to do the only thing possible – win her back. He would date her again, as if for the first time, and seek to win her heart a second time. They spent lots of time together talking, getting to know each other, and creating new memories. He was determined that she would get to know him all over again, fall in love with him again, and commit to be his wife a second time, and have memories of a wedding day. After almost 3 years, Kim finally proposed a second time, they were married again not long after. To Krickitt, this was something new, but to her husband it was God's gift in allowing his wife to get to know him and fall in love with him twice. Kim thanked God for allowing his wife to know him and love him all over again.[14]

Think of your best friends. How well do they know you? How well do you know them? I'm sure you know them pretty well, if they are your best friends. There is a safety and security that comes from being "known completely" by someone. In the context of marriage, being known and loved completely and intimately is definitely one of the greatest riches God gives. However, allowing yourself to be <u>known</u> by someone without the safety and security of marriage leaves the door open for hurt and destruction.

So what exactly does it mean to be "known"?

Now in the sixth month the angel Gabriel was sent by God to a city of Galilee named Nazareth, to a virgin betrothed to a man whose name was Joseph, of the house of David. The virgin's name was Mary. And having come in, the angel said to her, "Rejoice, highly favored one, the Lord is with you; blessed are you among women!" But when she saw him, she was troubled at his saying, and considered what manner of greeting this was. Then the angel said to her, "Do not be afraid, Mary, for you have found favor with God. And behold, you will conceive in your womb and bring forth a Son, and shall call His name JESUS. He will be great, and will be called the Son of the Highest; and the Lord God will give Him the throne of His father David. And He will reign over the house of Jacob forever, and of His kingdom there will be no end." Then Mary said to the angel, "How can this be, since I do not <u>know</u> a man?" And the angel answered and said to her, "The Holy Spirit will come upon you, and the power of the Highest will overshadow you; therefore, also, that Holy One who is to be born will be called the Son of God (Luke 1:26-35 NKJV, emphasis added).

Here we have the well-known Scripture that describes how the angel Gabriel announced to Mary that she would be the mother of the Messiah.

Question 1. According to the above verses, what is Mary's response to Gabriel when she learns she is going to have a baby? Write it here.

Mary questions Gabriel by responding that she does not know a man. Gabriel then assures her and tells her that the Holy Spirit Himself will come upon her, thereby making Jesus the Son of God.

Let's look at Mary's question in a little more detail. She states she does not know a man. At first this may seem like an odd statement for her to be making, after all, she is engaged to Joseph! How can she be engaged to a man if she does not know any men? Well, that's not what she means.

The key is that 'to know a man' takes on a completely different meaning here. In this case it does not mean the same thing as knowing someone like a friend, relative or even a person in the news. The phrase 'to know a man (or woman)' is a Jewish idiom that indicates *having sexual relations* with that person. In other translations such as the NIV, verse 34 is actually written to have Mary clearly say, "I am a virgin."

Turning back to our first couple, Adam and Eve, we see this same meaning in Genesis 4:1:
And Adam <u>knew</u> Eve his wife; and she conceived, and bore Cain, and said, "I have gotten a man from the LORD" (emphasis added).

Why is this so important? When a man and a woman engage in sexual activity, they <u>know</u> each other in a deep, intimate way that no other man or woman can or should know. Not only do they open themselves up physically by being naked, but they also expose and share deep emotions and feelings.

Remember yesterday we talked about being of one flesh, and completed in marriage? Being "known" is one of the great riches of God's plan and design for his children! This idea of a man and woman "knowing" each other in a way no one else does, falls right in line with the two flesh becoming one. In order for this to occur, there has to be something that binds these two separate individuals together so they are one. This unity is formed through sexual intimacy.

Question 2. Please share below your thoughts and comments on being known by another. Is this something you look forward to? Why?

Question 3. If a guy or girl is urging you to have sex before you are committed to them in marriage, are they realistically seeking to "complete" you and be "known" by you in the most productive, most beneficial and purest way possible?
Yes   No

The answer to Question 3 is <u>NO.</u> Not only is that kind of sex outside of God's parameters of marriage, but it also doesn't fulfill some of the best parts of that kind of intimate relationship. So consider what you're giving up before you give in to it.

We're not attempting to "scare you into purity," although the reality is that sinning by becoming involved sexually before marriage ought to scare you. God's wrath is by far the worst thing anyone could ever experience. There are blessings for those who wait to enjoy sexual intimacy with their marriage partner, and the wrath of God for those who give in to the demands of their flesh to be sexually active apart from marriage.

Question 4. Have you given in and sinned sexually in the past? If the answer is yes, have you confessed your sin to God and asked for forgiveness, both from God and from the one with whom you were sexually active?

If you have, then you can rejoice in the **REALITY** that God, the King has forgiven you and you are pure again – washed white as snow! If you have confessed your sin and been forgiven, you are free to pursue the riches and blessings God has in store for you with a pure relationship! God's forgiveness is amazing and wonderful for us all!

Question 5. How does this lesson shape your thoughts and views on sexuality and purity?

Scriptures to Consider

The body is not meant for sexual immorality, but for the Lord, and the Lord for the body. By his power God raised the Lord from the dead, and he will raise us also. Do you not know that your bodies are members of Christ himself? Shall I then take the members of Christ and unite them with a prostitute? Never! Do you not know that he who unites himself with a prostitute is one with her in body? For it is said, "The two will become one flesh." But he who unites himself with the Lord is one with him in spirit. Flee from sexual immorality. All other sins a man commits are outside his body, but he who sins sexually sins against his own body. Do you not know that your body is a temple of the Holy Spirit, who is in you, whom you have received from God? You are not your own; you were bought at a price. Therefore honor God with your body (1 Corinthians 6:13-20).

Did you live sexually pure today?
      Yes   *No*

Are you committed to staying sexually pure?
      Yes   *No*

DAY 15
Well, Wait!

In the previous lessons, we've discussed the subject of <u>marriage</u> in respect to sexuality. In particular we discussed that marriage is a lifelong commitment between the man and the woman. Remember it is only in this arrangement that sexuality can take on its deepest expression and meaning when two become one. It is only in this bond that a person can truly and fully be known, be completed and enjoy all the riches of intimacy.

At this stage in your life however, you are faced with a challenge – virginity. A virgin is a person who hasn't had sexual intercourse. There are a number of forces working on you right now, both internally and externally: hormones and adolescence, friends, a deeper attraction to the opposite sex, the boldness of media and sex in society, and so on — all of which may be influencing you to give up your virginity.

In this lesson we will talk through virginity and its importance, its value and its benefits. We will also talk about recovery strategies if it's already lost. But we will look a little deeper than just the "rules" and talk though a deeper issue. It's the issue of **waiting**.

Waiting is a difficult thing no matter what your age. (I know you all agree!) Waiting for your turn with a toy when you're 3, waiting for school to <u>begin</u> when you're 5, waiting for school to <u>end</u> when you're 18, waiting for spring to come when it's January, waiting for someone to ask you to the prom, waiting for the coach to call you off the bench, waiting for the one you will marry, waiting for sex, waiting for kids, waiting for grandkids… waiting never ends! It is so, so important… and I mean so, so, so important that you learn how to **wait**… and how to wait well! If you do not know how to wait, it will make your life full of frustration, impatience, unhappiness and bad decisions.

But those who wait on the Lord shall renew their strength; they shall mount up with wings like eagles, they shall run and not be weary, they shall walk and not faint (Isaiah 41:31 NKJV).

Question 1. According to Isaiah 41:31 above, what qualities are produced by waiting on the Lord?

Webster defines waiting as:
1. to stay for; to rest or remain stationary in expectation or anticipation of; as to wait orders to march.
2. to remain temporarily undone or neglected;
3. to be on the watch; to be on one's guard
4. to be ready or at hand

Be patient, then, brothers, until the Lord's coming. See how the farmer waits for the land to yield its valuable crop and see how patient he is for the autumn and spring rains. You too, be patient and stand firm, because the Lord's coming is near (James 5:7, 8).

Question 2. In waiting, what does James 5:7, 8 tell us to do? (beginning of both verses)

"When God brings a time of waiting," advised Oswald Chambers, "don't fill it with busyness, just wait." Usually we take the opposite approach because at times, waiting causes us to feel awkward, unproductive and even useless. From God's perspective, however, waiting deepens and widens our soul. [15] Waiting has no association with instant-fixes. Waiting requires patient perseverance with confident trust that God will provide the meaning and the conclusion in His perfect timing.

Waiting requires patience. John Piper describes patience as a "deepening, ripening, peaceful willingness to wait for God in the **unplanned place** of obedience, and to walk with God at the **unplanned pace** of obedience." [16] That's so hard! Many times we're willing to wait if it's convenient for our schedules and comfort. "Okay God, I'll wait for your leading, but I need a prom date by next week." "I'll wait Lord, but if you don't do something by 9:00 p.m., those internet pictures are just too addicting." "I am waiting Lord, so why haven't I met my husband yet?" Wait in the unplanned **place** and at the unplanned **pace**. "Be still and know that I am God." (Psalm 46:10)

Question 3. What things are you waiting for right now?

Question 4. What might God still want to do in YOU before bringing about the answer to your waiting? What does God want to teach you about Himself?

So how does purity and virginity relate to all this? Yes, we should seek to maintain our purity because He is pure. But purity and virginity are also extreme extensions of your ability to be patient and wait for the great riches God has. Waiting is not "the thing" today. Everything is quicker, faster, immediate and less hassle – and much of that is great! We all love our high speed Internet! But that mindset does not apply to everything, especially purity and virginity. In fact, purity and virginity are exactly the opposite of the immediate, self-satisfying desires within us. So is waiting. So please learn to wait well.

Waiting is beneficial in many ways. Learn to focus on the benefits of waiting, rather than the struggles of it.

Read the following verses about waiting: (NKJV- emphasis added)

Wait on the LORD; be of good courage, and He shall strengthen thy heart. Wait, I say, on the LORD! (Psalm 27:14).

Lead me in Thy truth and teach me, for Thou are the God of my salvation; on Thee do I wait all the day (Psalm 25:2).

Rest in the LORD and wait patiently for Him; fret not thyself because of him who prospereth in his way (Psalm 37:7).

My soul, wait silently for God alone, for my expectation is from Him (Psalm 62:5).

The LORD is good unto them that wait for Him, to the soul that seeketh Him (Lamentations 3:25).

It is good that a man should both hope and quietly wait for the salvation of the LORD (Lamentations 3:26).

So you, by the help of your God, observe mercy and justice, and wait on your God continually (Hosea 12:6).

Therefore I will look unto the LORD; I will wait for the God of my salvation; my God will hear me Micah 7:7).

But if we <u>hope</u> for what we do not see, we eagerly wait for it with <u>perseverance</u> (Romans 8:25).

Question 5. Which verse(s) stand out to you the most? Why?

So is waiting a completely passive process?

I wait for the Lord, my soul waits, and in His word I do hope. My soul waits for the Lord more than watchmen wait for the morning, yes, more than watchmen wait for the morning (Psalm 130:5,6).

There is an **active role** in waiting. We can become watchmen. In biblical times, watchmen vigilantly guarded the city. They watched for enemies who might move in at night and attack when the sun came up. They were alert and obedient, ready to respond when needed. When called upon, they sprang into action. But on the other hand, watchmen didn't make things happen. They didn't control the rising of the sun. They didn't try to speed up the process. A watchman knew the difference between his job and God's job.[17]

Question 6. List some character traits that may have been required of men who were given the job of a watchman in David's time.

Question 7. As you also wait and watch for what you desire in your future, what character traits need strengthened or maintained in your life?

You know, virginity is difficult, purity is difficult, and waiting is difficult. But the choices we make depend on what we are willing to settle for in life. Will you give up enduring, waiting and pursuing purity just because it's hard? Do you give up running and practicing for the coach because it's hot? No way – if you ever want to play in the game later!

Virginity and purity have all kinds of blessing and benefits. Virginity is important to strive to maintain so that your future marriage will be free from doubts, guilt, and fears. Virginity promotes and protects the riches of pure intimacy, oneness, and knowledge with one person someday in marriage. There are all kinds of positive things about virginity, and no doubt you've heard plenty of them. But

the key issue is **waiting**. **Do you know how to wait? Have you been waiting?**
Or have you been making things happen the way you want them to be, and taking
control of things yourself instead of trusting God with the timing? Will you
choose to wait well and patiently for the Lord to lead, direct and control your
life?

As we talk of virginity, know this: if you have already given up your virginity,
God is faithful and just to forgive us of our sins and cleanse us from all
unrighteousness (I John 1:9). You can begin again and be pure again. Confess
your sin to the Lord and then enjoy the immensity of His love and forgiveness!
Look at the story of a woman who Jesus did not condemn but washed her clean
and gave her new life.

But Jesus went to the Mount of Olives. At dawn he appeared again in the temple
courts, where all the people gathered around him, and he sat down to teach them.
The teachers of the law and the Pharisees brought in a woman caught in adultery.
They made her stand before the group and said to Jesus, "Teacher, this woman
was caught in the act of adultery. In the Law Moses commanded us to stone such
women. Now what do you say?" They were using this question as a trap, in order
to have a basis for accusing him.

But Jesus bent down and started to write on the ground with his finger. When
they kept on questioning him, he straightened up and said to them, "If any one of
you is without sin, let him be the first to throw a stone at her." Again he stooped
down and wrote on the ground.   At this, those who heard began to go away
one at a time, the older ones first, until only Jesus was left, with the woman still
standing there. Jesus straightened up and asked her, "Woman, where are they?
Has no one condemned you?"

"No one, sir," she said. "Then neither do I condemn you," Jesus declared. "Go
now and leave your life of sin" (John 8:1-11).

That day, the woman's life was turned around. She became a changed person
forever. How did it happen? There are two major things we can learn from her.
The first lesson can be found in <u>who</u> she stood before. Society and its leaders
were ready to condemn the woman and end her life. But as she stood before
Jesus, with her sin exposed, she was given a new life. She could not hide her sin
from Jesus, and instead of condemnation, she was commanded to live – and live
in a new way! Placing yourself before Jesus, with your sin exposed, is humbling
but will allow for new life to begin.

A second lesson can be learned by how Jesus told her to live. He said, *"Go
now and leave your life of sin."*   A key to being pure in heart is <u>repentance</u>.
Repentance literally means turning from our sin and walking in the opposite

direction. Jesus was telling her how to live from that day on, and it was opposite from how she had been living. Living a daily life of repentance — walking away from our sins and toward Jesus — is vital in cultivating a pure heart and pure life. If you have already given up the precious gift of your virginity, know that you can be purified and begin walking in another direction. Your heart will be cleansed from all unrighteousness… and you will be purified! Read 1 John 1:9 again and thank God for His promises and the hope it gives. If we confess our sins, he is faithful and just and will forgive us our sins and purify us from all unrighteousness (1 John 1:9)

So whether you are a virgin now, or whether you have been forgiven by Christ's grace, here's the more important question: **Will you choose to WAIT from this day on for God's best for you?** (That includes when you're a grandpa or grandma!) Seek God actively, and wait patiently in your spirit for what He has in store! Its riches will be beyond your imagination!

> **16-year-old Jim writes:** When I have a child, I want him/her to see that their parents love each other, that having a wonderful relationship with a spouse after many years is possible. I want my kid to think that I was 'cool' and that I didn't have to drink, party or fool around with girls to do so. The biggest thing I want is for my child to accept Jesus, that is above everything else. We heard a Bible study the other day at Fellowship of Christian Athletes and it talked about how it's important that when I have a child, that he can ask me, "Did you stay pure in marriage"' and I can say "Yes, I did, I waited for your mom."

Scriptures to Consider

If you , O LORD, kept a record of sins, O Lord, who could stand? But with you there is forgiveness; therefore you are feared. I wait for the LORD, my soul waits, and in his word I put my hope. My soul waits for the Lord more than watchmen wait for the morning, more that watchmen wait for the morning. O Israel, put your hope in the LORD, for with the LORD is unfailing love and with him is full redemption (Psalm 130:3-7, NIV.)

Did you live sexually pure today?
     Yes   *No*

Are you committed to staying sexually pure?
     Yes   *No*

DAY 16
God's Will

Have you ever wondered about God's Will for your life? Well, today we are going to explore this topic. We will be considering the following questions: What is the will of God for our lives? How do we find it? How do we do it? And what does that have to do with sexual purity?

What is God's Will for our Lives?

Read these verses and answer the questions below in order to get a clear picture of God's will.

¹Finally, brothers, we instructed you how to live in order to please God, as in fact you are living. Now we ask you and urge you in the Lord Jesus to do this more and more. ²For you know what instructions we gave you by the authority of the Lord Jesus.

³It is God's will that you should be sanctified: that you should avoid sexual immorality; ⁴that each of you should learn to control his own body in a way that is holy and honorable, ⁵not in passionate lust like the heathen, who do not know God; ⁶and that in this matter no one should wrong his brother or take advantage of him. The Lord will punish men for all such sins, as we have already told you and warned you. ⁷For God did not call us to be impure, but to live a holy life. ⁸Therefore, he who rejects this instruction does not reject man but God, who gives you his Holy Spirit (1 Thessalonians 4:1-8).

Question 1. In the passage above, Paul (the writer) talks about avoiding sexual immorality, controlling our bodies, and living a holy life. But before he mentions all this, he tells us why he instructs us how to live. What is the motive that he stated in verse 1?

Question 2. According to verse 3 above, what is the will of God?
 A. To be sanctified
 B. To be satisfied
 C. To be sacrifice

A Big Word!

Yes, it is bigger than a four-letter word, and it is probably not a word you use daily in your conversations with friends. But the word "sanctified" is very important to understand because it is God's Will for your life. So what does it mean?

Webster's Dictionary defines"sanctify" this way:
1. to be made holy;
2. to free from sin; to purify.

What is the Bible's definition of the word? Let's look at the rest of the verse 3 above (after the colon), and note the list of meanings attached to the word "sanctified". Paul (the writer) explains "sanctified" by saying: *a) avoid sexual immorality; b) learn to control your body in a holy and honorable way; c) don't do wrong to, or take advantage of a brother.* (By saying "brother" here he doesn't only mean a real, blood brother and to wrong a neighbor or friend is okay. He's talking to the family of believers, and as children of God we are brothers and sisters. Doing wrong or taking advantage of a fellow believer or any other person in an impure way goes against God's will and desire for your life.) So understanding the word "sanctified" is a key to knowing God's will for your life.

Question 3. Please write the definition of "sanctified" in your own words.

Our Motives for Purity

If we know God's Will is for us to be sanctified (holy, free from sin, pure), then our motives for living a pure life should flow from that understanding of God's will. By living out God's Will for our lives, we are pleasing God!

There are many good reasons why we should avoid sexual immorality and learn to control our bodies. However, if we are Christians, our primary motivation for pursuing purity should be so that we might better know and please the Lord. By living "sanctified" by God, we are pleasing to Him! Before we knew Jesus Christ we lived to please ourselves in ever-increasing wickedness, but now God's grace has changed our hearts so that we earnestly desire to please Him instead of ourselves. A sincere desire to please Him will drive us on to resist the Devil, to daily die to the temptations of our flesh, to forsake the pleasure of sin continually, to avoid sexual immorality and to control our bodies in a way that is holy and honorable. Our motive for purity should be to live in order to please God! (1 Thessalonians 4:1).

Question 4. Take a second and review your motives. Why are you pursuing purity, and avoiding sexual impurity?

The More and More Principle

Understanding the will of God and doing it are closely related, but they are two different things. You may have the head knowledge of what God's will is, but your actions may not live out what you know God desires. So let's take the knowledge of God's will to the next step. Let's learn how to do it.

Read 1 Thessalonians 4:1 again from the beginning of this lesson. How does Paul ask and urge us to do this (live to please God)? The answer lies in the last three words of verse 1. Paul says, "Now we ask you and urge you in the Lord Jesus to do this more and more." This is an important part of the instructions. Paul doesn't ask them to do it once, or even twice. But he asks and even urges them to do it more and more. When you do something more and more what usually happens? If you play basketball and your coach tells you to shoot 50 free-throws every day, what happens to your ability to shoot free-throws? If you play an instrument and your teacher requires you to practice every day, how is your playing affected? When you first learn to type on the computer, finding and punching one key at a time takes forever. But what happens to your typing ability when you spend hours and hours at the computer? There is a definite increase when you do something more and more. **What you choose to do more and more is what will increase.** That is the "more and more principle". If you choose to shoot free-throws, it is not your golf swing that will improve; it's your free-throw accuracy! If you practice an instrument, it's not your math grade that gets better. Instead, you become so familiar with the music you could probably play it from memory! Whatever you do "more and more" will be dramatically affected!

But the key question to ask yourself is, "What am I doing more and more"? If you eat doughnuts and ice cream every meal, every day (and you're never sick of it), the "more and more" principle has a negative affect on your body. Are you living in order to please God more and more, as Paul instructed in the verse above, or are you ignoring God, skipping church, living for your own pleasure more and more?

Be careful about offering yourself to sexual impurity of any kind. For when you offer yourself to the wrong thing, more and more, you will soon find that the enslavement process begins to increase. You'll want "more and more," and you'll continually seek something new and different to try to satisfy yourself.

> **Course Member Paul writes:** My lust pulled me deeper and deeper into more risqué and perverted activities. After awhile the women were not as exciting as before and I found myself drifting into homosexual activity. This was something that would have repulsed me before I became caught in the cycle of more and more.

Learning to do God's will is something that must be practiced more and more. The Christian life is one of ongoing improvement; growing in purity, increasing in holiness, abounding in the work of the Lord "more and more." If you are not living to please God more and more, then you are living to please yourself more and more.

Read these verses again and watch for some practical ways we can live to please God more and more.
¹Finally, brothers, we instructed you how to live in order to please God, as in fact you are living. Now we ask you and urge you in the Lord Jesus to do this more and more. ²For you know what instructions we gave you by the authority of the Lord Jesus.
³It is God's will that you should be sanctified: that you should avoid sexual immorality; ⁴that each of you should learn to control his own body in a way that is holy and honorable, ⁵not in passionate lust like the heathen, who do not know God; ⁶and that in this matter no one should wrong his brother or take advantage of him. The Lord will punish men for all such sins, as we have already told you and warned you. ⁷For God did not call us to be impure, but to live a holy life. ⁸Therefore, he who rejects this instruction does not reject man but God, who gives you his Holy Spirit. (1 Thessalonians 4:1-8).

Question 5. According to 1 Thessalonians 4:3 (written above) what are we to do with sexual immorality?
    A. Aggravate it
    B. Avoid it
    C. Accuse it

Question 6. According to verse 4 (written above) as Christians we must "learn something." What is it?
    A. We must learn to talk the right way.

B. We must learn how to get people to make a decision for Christ.

C. We must learn how to control our bodies in an honorable way.

Question 7. Verse 5 above describes those who live in "passionate lust." How are they described?

    A. People who don't know any better

    B. Heathen who do not know God

A crewman on a South Seas fishing vessel found himself in the kind of situation no one ever wants to be—swimming with sharks!

He was hired to process fish, but the cantankerous captain didn't think he was working fast enough. One day a school of sharks was following the boat, and in an outburst of anger the captain ordered his slow-working crewman thrown overboard! The hapless fellow swam as fast as he could, caught up with the ship, and was pulled on board.

This reminds me of a danger that we face as believers. Once in a while, we may find ourselves unexpectedly thrown into a situation where temptations are "swimming" all around us--at a business convention, at school, at a party, in a dormitory, or even in the workplace--and temptation seems overwhelming. We are in real danger. In a spiritual sense, we're "swimming with the sharks."

When that happens, our best option is to "flee" temptation and choose to do what is right (2 Timothy 2:22). That may mean physically leaving a place or situation as fast as possible (Genesis 39:12). In any case, we need to reach out to God, calling on Him for help and protection--so we don't become shark food. --DCE [18]

In the verses we read earlier, Paul is instructing Christians to live not like their pagan neighbors who did not know God. The pagans lived their lives in lust, giving in to the cravings of the flesh in sexual immorality, and the degrading of their bodies in sexual perversion. The pagans not only "swam with sharks" they were sharks! Don't live like them. Don't even swim among them for a while. You will get bitten sooner or later.

Paul's description of these people as those "who do not know God" is significant here. Knowing God, that is, having an intimate relationship with Him is the key ingredient that will enable us to "escape the corruption in the world caused by evil desires" (2 Peter 1:4), and give us the motivation to pursue purity.

Question 8. According to 1 Thessalonians 4:6 above, what will God do to people who live like this?

    A. He will overlook their sins.

    B. He will punish them.

    C. He knows we are only human and He understands our weaknesses.

Question 9. 1 Thessalonians 4:7 states the "calling" of the Christian. What is it?
A. To convert others
B. To hold up the 10 commandments as the standard of God
C. To live a holy life and to be pure

Question 10. How are you doing with your calling?

Question 11. According to 1 Thessalonians 4: 8 above, when people reject the teaching about avoiding immorality and learning to control their bodies, and about future punishment of those who continue to live in sin, what are they really rejecting?
A. They are rejecting the person who brings the message.
B. They are rejecting the teaching of men.
C. They are rejecting God!

Let us summarize the teaching of the above passage of Scripture:

What is God's will for our lives? **That we should be sanctified: that we should avoid sexual immorality; that we should learn how to control our bodies in a way that honors the Lord; that we should not wrong or take advantage of another.** That gives us a clearer understanding of specific choices we need to make everyday. Those individual choices we make every day lead to the more and more principle. We will either increase in godliness or increase in godlessness. By living more and more to please God instead of to please yourself, you are doing the Will of God. And that is so pleasing to Him!

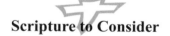

Scripture to Consider

You will be secure, because there is hope; you will look about you and take your rest in safety. You will lie down, with no one to make you afraid, and many will court your favor. But the eyes of the wicked will fail, and escape will elude them; their hope will become a dying gasp (Job 11:18-20).

Did you live sexually pure today?
       Yes   *No*

Are you committed to staying sexually pure?
       Yes   *No*

DAY 17

Radical Amputation

Today is KEY in your pursuit of purity, so you will want to absorb this lesson. We will refer back to it often, since it sets the stage for dealing with some of the sin we will talk about in the days to come. Remember who you are: adopted heirs of God, designed by God, royalty because of Jesus Christ and His sacrifice for you. This is a <u>radical</u> lesson today, but one that will help you daily for the rest of your life. Please pray to listen and learn well today. This lesson is for those committed to purity.

In the process of growth as a Christian, we need to cut away everything that hinders and separates us from God and His will for our lives. Read this Scripture and then we will talk about it.

If your hand causes you to sin, cut it off. It is better for you to enter life maimed than with two hands to go into hell, where the fire never goes out. And if your foot causes you to sin, cut it off. It is better for you to enter life crippled than to have two feet and be thrown into hell. And if your eye causes you to sin, pluck it out. It is better for you to enter the kingdom of God with one eye than to have two eyes and be thrown into hell (Mark 9:43-47).

Question 1. According to Mark 9 above, what is Jesus' remedy for that which causes you to sin?

Question 2. Does Jesus' remedy or method sound reasonable or radical?

It is a necessity to separate ourselves <u>completely</u> from whatever is causing, or has caused us to sin. Does this seem reasonable? There is no reasonable way to deal with unreasonable sin. Sin doesn't listen to reason. It is deceptive. It runs wild and rampant. It lies, because it is from Satan, the father of lies. Our dealing with sin must go beyond reasoning and instead be radical.

Jesus said that we should "cut off" and "pluck out" whatever causes us to sin, and He warned us that if we don't radically amputate the cause of our sin we could end up in hell. Do not take this lightly. We are talking life and death here; heaven and hell. If you thought you were "just playing" with impurity please know this: impurity, and all sin, will take you farther than you want to go, keep you longer than you want to stay, and cost you more than you want to pay.

Of course, Jesus is not referring to a physical cutting off of your foot or a plucking out of your eyeball. Blind men still lust. He's referring to the complete removal of the <u>causes</u> of your sin. He's saying that if we want to be free from certain sins, some things in our lives must go, and we must do whatever it takes. Maybe that means moving the computer into the kitchen, never watching TV alone, getting rid of the TV in your room or certain movies or CD's. Or maybe there's a certain skirt or shirt that's too short or too tight and only invites trouble. What do you need to eliminate? What do you need to amputate that is causing you to be led into impurity and sin?

In his book, *The Great Divorce*, C.S. Lewis gives us a good picture of the deception of sin and the need to be radical about amputating it. In his story, he and some others were on a bus trip that took them to the outskirts of heaven. There, they are able to get a glimpse of true reality about heaven and themselves. In this story, the people from the bus trip are "ghosts" for they are not fully human as they will be when they enter heaven for all eternity. And each "ghost" has something he must give up.

Read the following and see the "radicalness" of the amputation needed.

I saw coming towards us a Ghost who carried something on his shoulder. Like all the Ghosts, he was unsubstantial, but they differed from one another as smokes differ. Some had been whitish; this one was dark and oily. What sat on his shoulder was a little red lizard, and it was twitching its tail like a whip and whispering things in his ear. As we caught sight of him he turned his head to the reptile with a snarl of impatience. "Shut up, I tell you!" he said. It wagged its tail and continued to whisper to him. He ceased snarling, and presently began to smile. Then he turned and started to limp westward, away from the mountains.

"Off so soon?" said a voice. The speaker was more or less human in shape but larger than a man, and so bright that I could hardly look at him. His presence smote on my eyes and on my body too (for there was heat coming from him as well as light) like the morning sun at the beginning of a tyrannous summer day. "Yes, I'm off," said the Ghost. "Thanks for all your hospitality. But it's no good, you see. I told this little chap," (here he indicated the lizard), "that he'd have to be quiet if he came, which he insisted on doing. Of course his stuff won't do here: I realize that. But he won't stop. I shall just have to go home."

"Would you like me to make him quiet?" said the flaming Spirit – an angel, as I now understood.

"Of course I would," said the Ghost.

"Then I will kill him," said the Angel, taking a step forward.

"Oh – ah – look out! You're burning me. Keep away," said the Ghost retreating.

"Don't you want him killed?" said the Angel.

"You didn't say anything about killing him at first. I hardly meant to bother you with something so drastic as that."

"It's the only way," said the Angel, whose burning hands were now very close to the lizard. "Shall I kill it?"

"Well, that's a further question. I'm quite open to consider it, but it's a new point, isn't it? I mean, for the moment I was only thinking about silencing it..." said the Ghost.

"May I kill it?" asked the Angel.

"Well, there's time to discuss that later" said the Ghost.

"There is no time. May I kill it?"

"Please, I never meant to be such a nuisance. Please – really – don't bother. Look! It's gone to sleep of its own accord. I'm sure it will be all right now. Thanks ever so much."

"May I kill it?"

"Honestly, I don't think there's the slightest necessity for that. I'm sure I shall be able to keep it in order now. I think the gradual process would be far better than killing it." said the Ghost.

"The gradual process is of no use at all."

"Don't you think so? Well, I'll think over what you've said very carefully. I honestly will. In fact I'd let you kill it now, but as a matter of fact I'm not feeling frightfully well today. It would be silly to do it now. I'd need to be in good health for the operation. Some other day, perhaps."

"There is no other day. All days are present now."

"Get back! You're burning me. How can I tell you to kill it? You'd kill me if you did."

"It is not so."

"Why, you're hurting me now."

"I never said it wouldn't hurt you. I said it wouldn't kill you."...

The Angel's hands were almost closed on the Lizard, but not quite. Then the Lizard began chattering to the Ghost so loud that even I could hear what it was saying. "Be careful," it said. "He can do what he says. He can kill me. One fatal word from you and he will! Then you'll be without me forever and ever. It's not natural. How could you live? You'd only be a sort of ghost, not a real man as you are now. He doesn't understand. He's only a cold, bloodless abstract thing. It may be natural for him, but it isn't for us. Yes, yes. I know there are no real pleasures now, only dreams. But aren't they better than nothing? And I'll be so good. I admit I've sometimes gone too far in the past, but I promise I won't do it again. I'll give you nothing but really nice dreams – all sweet and fresh and almost innocent. You might say, quite innocent...."

"Have I your permission?" asked the Angel to the Ghost.

"I know it will kill me."

"It won't. But supposing it did?" asked the Angel

"You're right. It would be better to be dead than to live with this creature."

"Then I may?"

"...Go on, can't you! Get it over. Do what you like," bellowed the Ghost: but ended, whimpering, "God help me. God help me."

Next moment the Ghost gave a scream of agony such as I never heard on Earth. The Burning One closed his crimson grip on the reptile: twisted it, while it bit and writhed, and then flung it, broken backed on the turf.[19]

Some people, rather than cut off the causes of sin, want to stare it in the face and just say "no" or tell it to "be quiet" as C.S. Lewis described. They think that would be true victory. However, this desire to try to be <u>strong</u> rather than <u>pure</u> will not result in victory.

Question 4. Please list here what things have caused you to sin in the area of sexual impurity.

Question 5. Please list what "complete removal" would mean for you.

Question 6. Will you, today, totally "amputate" everything that has caused you to sin?

This is how you pursue purity with all your might! If something has already caused you to sin, get rid of it! It will only get worse! When you weigh the value of a computer or T.V. versus a happy, successful, God-blessed life, hopefully you can more easily prioritize what is most important to you.

There's an old man in our community who walked everywhere because he didn't have a car. He walked to church, walked to the store, walked to the restaurants. Because of a disease he had, one of his toes became infected. After a short time, gangrene set in and the doctors informed him that they must remove his infected toe. "Do what you have to do." he said.

The day after his surgery I visited him in the hospital and as I walked into the room I heard him laughing with his roommate and joking with his brother who was also visiting. He gave me a big hug and a huge grin and then went on to tell me how wonderful the nurses had been to him. A few minutes later, after watching his happiness, I just had to ask him, "Ronnie, you seem to be on top of the world; you don't seem sad about loosing your toe?"

He shot me a big toothy grin and said, "You know, my toe was diseased and even though it is only a small part of my body, if I had left it attached, the infection would have eventually killed me. So you see, sweetie, amputating that old diseased toe gave me my life back!

Are you hiding anything anywhere that can cause you to sin? If so, go throw it away. Get rid of it. Remember to see it in light of God's reality. Don't be fooled by the illusion that it won't hurt you again.

Therefore, since we are surrounded by such a great cloud of witnesses, let us throw off everything that hinders and the sin that so easily entangles, and let us run with perseverance the race marked out for us (Hebrews 12:1).

Question 6. According to Hebrews 12:1 above, what should we "throw off"?

Question 7. What is the difference between "throwing off" and "gently placing" something aside?

Question 8. In your own words, describe the principle of Radical Amputation that was taught today.

Scripture to Consider

The thief comes only to steal and kill and destroy; I have come that they may have life, and have it to the full (John 10:10).

Did you live sexually pure today?
        Yes   *No*

Are you committed to staying sexually pure?
        Yes   *No*

DAY 18
Radical Consumption

We have covered some heavy topics the last few days. We've dealt with the issue of radically amputating anything in your life that is not in line with the rich inheritance God has for you as heirs with Christ. Perhaps some of you have been brave and have amputated some things from your daily life already. Keep fighting the good fight! Maybe some of you will run into the need for radical amputation in the future. Whether for now or in the future, it is vitally important to understand the next step after radical amputation.

Once you amputate the false substitutes for God-blessed relationships, you must fill that huge hole with something. You must fill the hole and replace the removed areas with something strong, or you will collapse and fail even further, leaving a bigger mess.

At our house (Nathan & Jena) we recently dug up a beautiful bush in our front flowerbed. The bush had pretty little white flowers and was full and lush. However, for all its prettiness, the bush was also being overtaken by thistles! Not just small insignificant weeds, but big, thick, dense thistles – some taller than the bush itself! We tried to spray just the thistles without killing the bush, but they wouldn't die. We tried to dig them up but couldn't get deep enough to kill the roots. We tried just cutting them off so no one would see them, but the thistles always grew back faster and taller than the last time. So our only final option was to dig up the entire bush, thistles and all. When we were finished, the hole in front of our house was huge! But it was the only way to remove all the thistles! When we were finished, we were so tired that we put our tools away and went to bed talking about what an accomplishment it was to dig up all those thistles. By morning, however, our accomplishment had turned into quite the mess. It had rained overnight. Our huge hole was full of water, mud and a majority of the mulch we had carefully spread around other parts of the flowerbed. Recently planted flowers were also floating in the hole, as the water had eroded other parts of our flowerbed. The water was running underneath our front porch and headed toward the basement windows. What a mess! It was worse to look at than a pretty bush full of thistles! If we had taken the time to fill the hole with something else – dirt, mulch, another bush – rather than just leave it open and waiting to collect stuff, we could have avoided the even bigger mess we faced.

It's true with purity too. In your life, you must put something in place of what's been amputated. That's the reality to continuing on the path of purity. You must refill all the amputated areas with something. You must refill the holes with something strong, something pure, something healthy. You must radically consume something in place of what you've given up. The best thing to radically consume is Jesus Christ! He is called the Living Water. Filling up with Jesus will leave you more satisfied than anything else. You'll run out of strength, desire, AND motivation on your own. But allowing Jesus to give you the Living Water that he offers will so satisfy you that you will never be thirsty for anything else again. You **must** radically consume the Living Water in order to survive and ever be wholly satisfied and complete.

Please read through the following Biblical story found in John 4:7-30 and answer the questions below.

[7] When a Samaritan woman came to draw water, Jesus said to her, "Will you give me a drink?" [8] (His disciples had gone into the town to buy food.) [9] The Samaritan woman said to him, "You are a Jew and I am a Samaritan woman. How can you ask me for a drink?" (For Jews do not associate with Samaritans.) [10] Jesus answered her, "If you knew the gift of God and who it is that asks you for a drink, you would have asked him and he would have given you living water." [11] "Sir," the woman said, "you have nothing to draw with and the well is deep. Where can you get this living water? [12] Are you greater than our father Jacob, who gave us the well and drank from it himself, as did also his sons and his flocks and herds?"
[13] Jesus answered, "Everyone who drinks this water will be thirsty again, [14] but whoever drinks the water I give him will never thirst. Indeed, the water I give him will become in him a spring of water welling up to eternal life." [15] The woman said to him, "Sir, give me this water so that I won't get thirsty and have to keep coming here to draw water." [16] He told her, "Go, call your husband and come back." [17] "I have no husband," she replied. Jesus said to her, "You are right when you say you have no husband. [18] The fact is, you have had five husbands, and the man you now have is not your husband. What you have just said is quite true." [19] "Sir," the woman said, "I can see that you are a prophet…"

In the above story, Jesus Christ spoke to a woman about two kinds of water:

1. **"This water,"** which would not satisfy and would not quench thirst. The woman would have to keep coming back again and again to the well to get more of "this water."

2. **"The water I give,"** which would quench thirst eternally.

Then Jesus brought up the fact that the woman had had multiple relationships (5 husbands and a current live-in—6 total). Obviously, she was finding no permanent satisfaction in these relationships so she had to keep going back to find a new love, each time hoping that this time would be the last. In bringing up her "unquenchable thirst" for different relationships, Jesus revealed to her that she would never be truly satisfied until she began "drinking" from the water He would give her.

Question 1. List the "water" from which you've been drinking and how it has left you "thirsty."(What are some things with which you have tried to satisfy yourself, and what was the result?)

Question 2. What did Jesus mean when He said, "Everyone who drinks this water will be thirsty again"?
   A. The water in that well contained a high amount of salt.
   B. Ongoing sinful relationships (sexual impurity) will not ultimately satisfy, and will have to be repeated over and over.

Question 3. What kind of water did Jesus offer the woman at the well?
   A. Living Water
   B. Well water
   C. Tonic water

Question 4. What did Jesus say was the difference between the water she had been drinking and the living water He offered her?
   A. The Living Water was salt-free.
   B. The Living Water would satisfy.
   C. The Living Water had more nutrients.

Question 5. What did Jesus say the effects of drinking this water would be?
   A. More energy and stamina
   B. Lower cholesterol
   C. Eternal life

Jesus offered this woman Living Water. He said that if she drank it she would not be thirsty anymore; in other words, she would be satisfied and not desire one relationship after another. Here is hope for you and me! Here is the method to purity. Radically consume this Living Water. If you discover how to consume this "living water," and how to drink it radically, you will not be thirsty for less satisfying things anymore; in other words, you will be free from the craving of and slavery to any habitual sin.

Question 6. Please describe how this teaching is giving you hope. How can drinking this water satisfy you and change the way you live? Be specific.

> **Course member Simon writes:** Before, I was trying to quit viewing pornography mainly on my own strength, without replacing my thirst with the Living Water Christ supplies. Now I believe I can leave it all behind, because Jesus is really helping me. By drinking the Living Water Jesus gives, a satisfying, fulfilling water, I believe I can be free. The difference this time is the Living Water. Without that, I couldn't quit. With it, I can't help quitting.

Practically Speaking

What does it mean to "drink the living water"? What does it actually look like daily to be satisfied with Jesus Christ? How does radically consuming Christ enable us to leave sin behind? Let's discuss some practicalities of how all this looks.

Practical Drinking

What does it mean to drink the Living Water? It can be as basic as reading the Bible. However, be careful, it is possible to read the Bible and not drink of the living water. So how do we radically "drink" or consume the Living Water? Drinking implies taking something in to your system, and receiving nourishment and sustenance from it. I can read the words that say Jesus is Living Water and yet not drink of Him. Drinking is directly related to the application of Scripture in our lives, and it is much more of than mere reading. When you read the Scripture, ask God to apply it to your heart and to change your life by the reading of it. This is what it means to drink the Living Water. Let the living words of the Bible soak into your heart so that it affects your daily life.

Let's try it. Consider this verse and then put yourself in the scenario below:

For you make me glad by your deeds, O LORD; I sing for joy at the works of your hands. How great are your works, O LORD, how profound your thoughts! The senseless man does not know, fools do not understand, that though the wicked spring up like grass and all evildoers flourish, they will be forever destroyed. But you, O LORD, are exalted forever (Psalm 92:4-8).

Question 7. Suppose you read this verse before you left for school one morning. It was encouraging to you. However, on the way to school, your brother was acting like a jerk., Then when you arrived at school you realized you hadn't studied for your history test. You forgot your gym clothes at home, and now your best friend seems to like hanging out with someone else better than you. How can this verse you read in the morning help you in the kind of day you now find yourself? Think carefully and practically and please write your thoughts below. Here are some ideas to help get you started...

- Who is the focus of these verses?
- What about the Lord do these verses praise?
- What is the writer's <u>response</u> to the Lord in these verses?
- How can <u>you</u> apply these verses to your life today so they affect you?

Daily Satisfied

What does it look like in daily living to be <u>satisfied</u> in Christ? It means rejoicing in the love, forgiveness and grace of God on a daily basis, despite your circumstances. It is the response to the practical drinking we discussed above. It is discovering and learning more about Jesus Christ every day and being amazed and irresistibly drawn to him by what we discover. When we become "happy" in Jesus Christ we don't need to look for happiness in pornography, lust, food, or other things. This is the only sure means of avoiding impurity. Look at the scenario above again as an example and evaluate how well you are looking for ways to be "happy" or satisfied in God beyond all the external circumstances.

Drowning Out Sin

How does this radical consumption of Jesus Christ, the Living Water, actually enable us to leave sin behind? Simply put, if we are full and satisfied in Jesus Christ we don't need anything else. We are full, not thirsty for more and different ways to be satisfied. We are so saturated with the living water, that sin cannot get a foothold anywhere. How much of the living water are you drinking? Are you saturating yourself with it? Or, do you just taste it? Are you drinking so much that you are drowning out every possible area that sin can grow or are you sipping of other "water fountains" that nurture sin? There are so many other "water fountains". Each one promises satisfaction and delight, but none fully come through on that promise. Lust, pornography, alcohol, smoking, TV, money, relationships, gambling, drugs and other sin promise to satisfy. They are an invitation to drink of happiness some other temporary way, but they will never satisfy and only cause us to crave for more. Be radical in the way you consume Jesus Christ and his Word. He will help you enjoy the good things in life even more and He will help you drown out the sin that will destroy.

> **Morgan, age 15, writes:** I had fallen into sin a year ago, before coming to Setting Captives Free. I was suicidal to the point of being hospitalized for that year. Not only was I not accepting the life that my awesome God had given me, but I had also fallen into impurity. I became addicted to pornography and self-gratification.. God started to heal the suicidal part of me, and I was able to come back home, but the self-gratification and pornography just got worse. God moved me to join this course, and with God's help, and Setting Captives Free, I have started to break free of this sin! Wherever God is, there is love and hope! Take courage! Drink from the living water of Christ everyday, and the sin will wither away. God bless you all. You can break free from this sin.

Question 8. Are there other "fountains" in your life from which you have been drinking and looking for satisfaction? If so, what are they? List them here:

Then the angel showed me the river of the water of life, as clear as crystal, flowing from the throne of God and of the Lamb [2] down the middle of the great street of the city. On each side of the river stood the tree of life, bearing twelve crops of fruit, yielding its fruit every month. And the leaves of the tree are for the healing of the nations. [3] No longer will there be any curse (Revelation 22:1-3).

Question 9. According to the verse above, from where does the river of the water of life flow?

On the last and greatest day of the Feast, Jesus stood and said in a loud voice, "If anyone is thirsty, let him come to me and drink. Whoever believes in me, as the Scripture has said, streams of living water will flow from within him." By this he meant the Spirit, whom those who believed in him were later to receive (John 7:37-39).

Question 10. To whom did Jesus extend the invitation to come to Him and drink?

Question 11. What happens to those who believe in Him?

Question 12. Are you thirsty? Have you gone to him to drink yet today?

Scripture to Consider

"Teacher, which is the greatest commandment in the Law?" Jesus replied: "'Love the Lord your God with all your heart and with all your soul and with all your mind.' This is the first and greatest commandment. (Matthew 22:36-38).

Did you live sexually pure today?
       Yes   *No*

Are you committed to staying sexually pure?
       Yes   *No*

Notes

DAY 19
Radical Accountability

Today we will see the value and necessity of finding and maintaining an accountability partner.

Two are better than one, because they have a good return for their work: If one falls down, his friend can help him up. But pity the man who falls and has no one to help him up! Also, if two lie down together, they will keep warm. But how can one keep warm alone? Though one may be overpowered, two can defend themselves. A cord of three strands is not quickly broken (Ecclesiastes 4:9-12).

A study was conducted with horses to determine the true value of team effort. The study revealed that one horse pulling alone was able to pull 2,500 pounds. The test was then repeated with two horses pulling together; the two horses were able to pull 12,500 pounds! The two horses together were able to pull 5 times the amount of weight that the one horse alone could pull alone! That's synergy! That's the power of teamwork. Ecclesiastes 4:9 is about the power of synergy or teamwork in regard to spiritual fruit. Teamwork is critical in overcoming sexual sin and pursuing purity.

Question 1. Why are two better than one?

Course member Mike writes: "I was in bondage to pornography for 15 years, the last 10 of which were as a Christian. I kept my sins a secret because I was too proud to tell anyone else. But God brought me very low and then began teaching me the necessity of having an accountability partner. My wife and my pastor became my accountability partners. I've been totally free from all forms of pornography for years now. Two are better than one. My freedom and victory are intimately related to the accountability that has come into my life."

The trilogy "The Lord of the Rings" gives us several awesome pictures of accountability between two friends Sam and Frodo. As Frodo is burdened with carrying the evil Ring to its destruction, Sam is right beside him helping to make sure Frodo isn't overcome by the allurement of the evil Ring. Several times Sam proved his loyalty as he had to grab Frodo or shake him in order to snap him back into reality of their mission together and away from the lure of the power of the Ring. A favorite accountability scene, though, is found at the end of the movie as the two little hobbits are climbing Mt. Doom in the final steps of their quest to destroy the evil Ring. Frodo falls and being so faint from the journey and the evil he is battling, he cannot take another step. At that point, his friend and greatest accountability partner Sam tells him, "I can't carry the Ring for you, but I can carry you!" Sam hoists Frodo up onto his back and starts climbing the mountain with his friend, until Frodo can regain some strength. It's a great picture of avoiding failure and doom thanks to the power of accountability! You and I need friends and partners like Sam if we are to succeed in destroying the sin that wants to overcome us![20]

Question 2. Can you recall a time when you've "fallen" into sin and then had no strength to "get up?" What were the results? What happened? What did you do?

Brothers, if someone is caught in a sin, you who are spiritual should restore him gently. But watch yourself, or you also may be tempted (Galatians 6:1).

Question 3. We all need an accountability partner. From Galatians 6:1 above, what qualifications does an accountability partner need to possess in order to help?

Question 4. What about you? Have you had anyone come alongside and "help you pull more?" Have you had anyone "help you up" when you fell into impurity? If so, describe about that friend and how they helped hold you accountable.

But encourage one another, as long as it is called today, so that none of you may be hardened by sin's deceitfulness (Hebrews 3:13).

Question 5. Notice how "daily encouragement" is an antidote to sin. According to this verse, how often should you and your accountability partner communicate?

Getting Accountable

Think of someone you trust who loves God and will be your partner in this battle for purity. If a name or face doesn't come to mind immediately, begin praying now for God to bring you that friend. Having someone battle with you is essential to maintaining purity in your life. Once you have someone in mind who will help you in your quest for purity, you will need to find some time to talk to them about your need for accountability. This may not be easy, but it is vital. Plan out a time to discuss with your friend how this accountability between the two of you should look.

Here are some guidelines that will help as you pursue accountability with a friend:

1. **Agree to openness and honesty.** Bondage to sin brings deception with it; some of us have been deceptive for years. If we want to stop the slavery to sin it starts with honesty, even if it is humbling. No hiding. If your accountability partner asks how you are doing, and you have recently fallen into sin, you must honestly admit this. Otherwise, you are not allowing them to be your partner, and they cannot help pick you up if they don't know when you've fallen.

2. **Agree to prepare and share your plan** with your accountability partner to radically amputate sin and radically consume Christ. Allow your accountability partner to help you by making suggestions to your plan and holding you accountable to the specifics of it. Working together on this is a powerful key to its success.

3. **Agree to give your partner freedom to ask the hard questions**, without taking offense. Sometimes boldness will be needed as you battle for purity. Don't view your accountability partner as condemning you, but as asking the tough, blunt questions in order to get the full picture of where/how they can best help and love you.

4. **Agree to communicate about purity <u>daily</u>** for at least the first 30 days. Connect with your accountability partner, whether through email, telephone, at school, church or wherever. Commit to each other to connect on these deep important issues every day for a month to set the habit and also to fight the initial battles together, as they are sometimes the toughest.

5. **Accountability should be with a partner of the same gender.** It is not wise to desire accountability with someone who might provide further temptation for you. When considering accountability, consider making it with someone of the same sex.

6. **Finally, accountability should be initiated, and carried on, by the one desiring accountability**, not by the partner. In other words, if you desire accountability, you should take the initiative of contacting a partner, providing your reports, checking in often, etc. and not leave the initiative with the other person. Accountability is your responsibility and others should not be blamed if they do not follow through. You follow through with them, and all is well.

Read these verses again:
⁹Two are better than one, because they have a good return for their work: ¹⁰If one falls down, his friend can help him up. But pity the man who falls and has no one to help him up! ¹¹Also, if two lie down together, they will keep warm. But how can *one keep w*arm alone? ¹²Though one may be overpowered, two can defend themselves. A cord of three strands is not quickly broken (Ecclesiastes 4:9-12).

Two people working together can do several powerful things. They can produce spiritual **fruit** (vs. 9), they can provide spiritual **restoration** (vs. 10), prompt spiritual **fervor** (vs. 11), and they can provide spiritual **protection** (vs. 12).

Question 6. What four things do the verses above teach that "two together" can provide? Why are these important?

Question 7. Have any of these four qualities been missing in your life? Which ones?

To be honest, if you are unwilling to maintain an accountability relationship then most likely you will not win in your pursuit of purity for any length of time. Remember, *"one can be overpowered."* However, if you will contact a close friend, parents, or another, then *"two can defend themselves"* and you can experience victory! We are in a battle! There is no question about that fact. You can either be "overpowered" or you can "defend yourself," depending on your willingness to find a partner in the battle.

Notice this Biblical story that reinforces the truth we have been studying:

Joab saw that there were battle lines in front of him and behind him; so he selected some of the best troops in Israel and deployed them against the Arameans. He put the rest of the men under the command of Abishai his brother and deployed them against the Ammonites. Joab said, 'If the Arameans are too strong for me, then you are to come to my rescue; but if the Ammonites are too strong for you, then I will come to rescue you.' Be strong and let us fight bravely for our people and the cities of our God. The LORD will do what is good in his sight (2 Samuel 10:9-12).

The end result of this battle was victory for the Israelites. Joab in essence said, "You help me with my enemy and I'll help you with yours." And so together they were victorious, whereas separately they would have been conquered. This is an important aspect of an accountability relationship. We should provide one another with spiritual protection from our mutual enemy. The way we do this is to pray for each other, share "battle tips" that helped us, take each other to the Word of God, and help each other amputate the causes of sin. This is a winnable war. But it takes much more than you can do alone!

Scripture to Consider

Let us hold unswervingly to the hope we profess, for he who promised is faithful. And let us consider how we may spur one another on toward love and good deeds. Let us not give up meeting together, as some are in the habit of doing, but let us encourage one another—and all the more as you see the Day approaching (Hebrews 10:23-25).

As iron sharpens iron, so one man sharpens another (Proverbs 27:17).

Did you live sexually pure today?
     Yes   *No*

Are you committed to staying sexually pure?
     Yes   *No*

DAY 20
Purity Precedes Power

Many of those who believed now came and openly confessed their evil deeds. A number who had practiced sorcery brought their scrolls together and burned them publicly. When they calculated the value of the scrolls, the total came to fifty thousand drachmas. In this way the word of the Lord spread widely and grew in power (Acts 19:18-20).

There! Did you notice it? Immediately after Scripture records that the people "radically amputated" (burned) their books of sorcery, it tells us about the power that came. Read it again: "In this way the word of the Lord spread widely and grew in power!" Here is evidence that before power comes, purity must pave the way. Purity precedes power.

But now, let us examine one of the ways that the Devil keeps people enslaved to sexual impurity. He tries to put things backwards and make us think that power precedes purity. But power without purity can build pride, false security, and the "illusion" that we're okay without God and can make it on our own. Read this testimony:

> **From an Anonymous writer:** "I have not continued on in the course because I have been viewing pornography. In response to your advice that I 'cut off and throw away the CDROM' that has the porn on it I respond that it is not the CDROM that causes me to sin, it is my own heart. It would not be reasonable to cut off the CDROM and throw it away as I would just find something else to view. My idea of victory is to be able to have the CDROM nearby and say no to it. I will continue looking for another method of freedom."

This young man is looking to his own power in order to find purity. But he will not find power to "say no" until he radically amputates his sin and purifies his life. Can you see the illusion? He believes he has the power in himself to overcome sin. God says He will help us overcome, but He does not tell us to prove our power by remaining in the vicinity of sin.

So, if you think you are standing firm be careful that you don't fall! No temptation has seized you except what is common to man. And God is faithful; he will not let you be tempted beyond what you can bear. But when you are tempted, he will also provide a way out so that you can stand up under it (I Corinthians 10:12-14).

One of our mentors writes: "I've been meditating on this whole issue and thinking about how some of those testified that their strength against sin wasn't really being put to the test unless they stood when being faced with it. That is so unbiblical. God NEVER tells us to do that. He says, 'Flee'—Get out of there! Don't stick around! I believe that is yet another tactic of Satan to cause us to fall flat. I believe that it is only tempting/testing the goodness of God in His grace of past deliverance to be dumb enough to put myself back in the path of sin."

Warning: those who trifle with the clear teaching of God's Word that we are to deal radically with sin will not achieve lasting purity, will not perceive spiritual matters correctly, and will not receive God's power in their lives.

Why ask for trouble and cause your own downfall...? (2 Chronicles 25:19).

In the forests of northern Europe and Asia lives a little animal called the ermine, known for his snow-white fur in winter. He instinctively protects his white coat against anything that would soil it.

Fur hunters take advantage of this unusual trait of the ermine. They don't set a snare to catch him, but instead they find his home, which is usually a cleft in a rock or a hollow in an old tree. They smear the entrance and interior with grime. Then the hunters set their dogs loose to find and chase the ermine. The frightened animal flees toward home but doesn't enter because of the filth. Rather than soil his white coat, he is trapped by the dogs and captured while preserving his purity. For the ermine, purity is more precious than life.[21]

How precious is purity to you? If purity precedes power for God's people, how are you fighting for your purity?

Let's see a powerful demonstration of this truth taught in a story from the Bible. Here is the background: The Israelites had just won a great victory over the very fortified city of Jericho and were preparing for battle against the small town of Ai. They were not too concerned about the outcome of this battle because Ai was small. But they lost! They were humiliated. Notice why they lost:

Israel has sinned; they have violated my covenant, which I commanded them to keep. They have taken some of the devoted things; they have stolen, they have lied, they have put them with their own possessions. That is why the Israelites cannot stand against their enemies...You cannot stand against your enemies until you remove ...[whatever is devoted to destruction]! (Joshua 7:11-13, Explanation added).

God is saying that He will not be with them unless they destroy whatever is among them that is devoted to destruction. As it turns out, a man by the name of Achan took a "beautiful robe, two hundred shekels of silver and a wedge of gold..." (verse 21) from the victory at Jericho, and was cherishing and hiding them. But notice the words that God used to show why the Israelites lost the battle: "You can not stand against your enemies until you remove it...[whatever is devoted to destruction]."

This is vital in our pursuit of purity. Until we remove that which has caused us to sin we cannot expect power over the enemy. Purity precedes power. Notice what happens next:

Then Joshua, together with all Israel, took Achan, son of Zerah, the silver, the robe, the gold wedge, his sons and daughters, his cattle, donkeys and sheep, his tent and all that he had, to the Valley of Achor. Then all Israel stoned him, and after they had stoned the rest, they burned them.

Now that is radical amputation! It is removing that which has caused sin. Notice what happened next:

Twelve thousand men and women fell that day—all the people of Ai. So Joshua burned Ai and made it a permanent heap of ruins, a desolate place to this day (Joshua 8:25-28).

If we want to make sexual sins in our lives "a permanent heap of ruins—a desolate place" then we must cut off that which causes us to sin. Purity precedes power.

Question 1. Why did Israel lose the battle with Ai

    A. They were outnumbered

    B. They were unskilled in battle

    C. Achan was hiding items devoted to destruction.

Question 2. What did the Israelites do to the man who was cherishing and hiding items of destruction?

    A. They learned how to fight while he was still with them.

    B. They ignored him and kept fighting battles.

    C. They killed (amputated) him.

They not only removed Achan, but also his entire family, cattle, donkey, sheep and "all that he had." They stoned him, stoned the rest, and then burned them all. Now, definitely don't go out and stone or hurt another person. But here is truth that can apply to us. To become pure and powerful in battle we need to thoroughly destroy everything remotely connected to our previous bondage to sin. Stone it, burn it, and bury all of its "relatives." Then watch how powerful God makes us. Of course we're not talking about doing physical harm to other people. But sometimes we cherish our possessions more than purity. Can you be radical in removing "the door" by which impurity has entered your life? There is real strength in fighting to remove that which is causing your destruction.

Question 3. What did it take for the Israelites to have power in battle?
    A. It took learning new battle strategy
    B. Purity
    C. 3-a-day practices

There is a spiritual principle taught in the above passage that has everything to do with you and your fight for purity. If you will radically amputate anything that can trip you up, you will experience God fighting for you. Is there anything more important to you that you wouldn't willingly turn over in order to have God fighting for you? When you turn things over to God and amputate the avenues of sin, you will have power that results from purity. How important is purity to you?

Question 4. What do you need to amputate in order to have power in your life?

Question 5. Did you learn anything new in this lesson today? What are your thoughts?

Scripture for Today

Blessed are the pure in heart, for they will see God (Matthew 5:8).

Did you live sexually pure today?
    Yes   *No*

Are you committed to staying sexually pure?
    Yes   *No*

DAY 21
Intimacy

Contrary to popular media definition, the simple act of sex is not "the ultimate" between lovers. Does that surprise you? If it were, it would lessen the occurrence of divorce, pornography wouldn't be on the rise, and marriages would be more fulfilled by simply having sex. Although God did give us sex and intends it for enjoyment in marriage, He gave us something even greater— intimacy. Intimacy does not begin with the first kiss, it begins with the first conversation. Intimacy is not wrapped up in the first time you have sex, it is wrapped up in the deep knowledge and connection you have with another person. Intimacy is not pleasing yourself; it is caring so much about another that your greatest fulfillment is in seeing them fulfilled.

Learn about true intimacy now and seek only God to fulfill that in a future marriage partner. As you grow in your relationship with Christ, learn to recognize reality from illusion in intimacy. See true intimacy and don't be deceived by its imposter: lustful illusion.

In today's lesson we will look more deeply at how Satan has perverted God's plan of intimacy, and over the next few lessons we will look at specific examples of this perversion in our society. To begin, let's take a look at what it means to "pervert" something. The following definition is from Merriam-Webster's Collegiate Dictionary:

> 1a. to cause to turn aside or away from what is good or true or morally right : **to CORRUPT**
> 1b. to cause to turn aside or away from what is generally done or accepted : **to MISDIRECT**
> 2a. to divert to a wrong end or purpose : **to MISUSE**
> 2b. to twist the meaning or sense of : **to MISINTERPRET**

See those four key words: *corrupt, misdirect, misuse and misinterpret.* Those describe Satan's agenda. Therefore, when we speak of sexual perversion we are talking about those things that are outside God's plan for intimacy through sexuality. Satan is the master of perversion, and will try to twist anything good to make it evil in order to deceive God's people. This deception is why it is so important to have the Holy Spirit in us and God's Word in our hearts so we know truth and reality, and we will not be duped by Satan and his illusion! You must know what <u>reality</u> is to recognize illusion.

Question 1. To pervert something is to: (the four words from the definition above).

Question 2. The Master of Perversion is
A. John
B. Satan
C. The man at the porn store

Course member Nate writes: At first, I just wanted a girlfriend. I thought it would be fun to have someone to always spend time with and someone who would like me more than others. But once I had a girlfriend, and we saw so differently about so many things, I realized that it was more than simply a "girlfriend" I wanted, it was a deep friend. Looking back, it was intimacy I desired. I wanted someone I could share stuff with and she wouldn't think it was stupid. I wanted someone I didn't have to keep proving my strength to, because she believed in me. I wanted her to really believe that I was strong and had what it took to come through for her. Now that I'm married and have found the love of my life, I am amazed how awesome our intimacy is… not just the sex… but knowing and really being connected in heart with someone else who loves you so much and believes the best about you. I thank God for the intimate friendship He's given in my relationship with my wife. It's like nothing else in the world.

In the next few lessons, we want you to see the riches God creates for us, versus the sin we need to radically amputate. Intimacy is wonderful! It is part of the riches God has in store for us! See that reality! But also see how sexual intimacy in any way, shape or form outside of God's design of marriage is a perverted illusion from Satan and must be radically amputated or it will destroy.

Sexual sin takes on many forms, but each one in some way or another, goes against God's desire for true, pure intimacy between husband and wife. We will take a look at some of the hidden perversions. By this we mean those sinful acts that are not as visible in our society. Remember we want you to understand true intimacy God's way and also see the ways Satan tries to pervert our desire for intimacy.

122

Perversions of Intimacy

1. One type of perversion of sexual intimacy is called bestiality. This is sexual activity with animals. Not only is it impossible to have intimacy with animals, but it is also a mock on God's creation of intimacy. Here's straight reality of what the Bible says about bestiality:

Do not have sexual relations with an animal and defile yourself with it. A woman must not present herself to an animal to have sexual relations with it; that is a perversion (Leviticus 18:23).

Anyone who has sexual relations with an animal must be put to death (Exodus 22:19).

Question 3. In Leviticus 18:23, what does God call sexual relations with animals?

Question 4. Also according to Leviticus 18:23, what do we do to ourselves if we conduct such activity?

Question 5. In Exodus 22:19, what does God say is to happen to someone who has had sexual relations with an animal?

Question 6. How strong would you say God's hatred is for the perversion of intimacy in this way?

Bestiality is a perversion of God's design for intimacy. If you have any dealings in this area, radically amputate, and then run to Jesus to correct your view of intimacy through a true relationship with Him!

The second perversion of sexual intimacy we will discuss is incest, or sex between family members. The Bible gives us some strong words on this topic as well.

No one is to approach any close relative to have sexual relations. I am the LORD.
Do not dishonor your father by having sexual relations with your mother. She is your mother; do not have relations with her.
Do not have sexual relations with your father's wife; that would dishonor your father.
Do not have sexual relations with your sister, either your father's daughter or your mother's daughter, whether she was born in the same home or elsewhere.
Do not have sexual relations with your son's daughter or your daughter's daughter; that would dishonor you.
Do not have sexual relations with the daughter of your father's wife, born to your father; she is your sister.
Do not have sexual relations with your father's sister; she is your father's close relative.
Do not have sexual relations with your mother's sister, because she is your mother's close relative.
Do not dishonor your father's brother by approaching his wife to have sexual relations; she is your aunt.
Do not have sexual relations with your daughter-in-law. She is your son's wife; do not have relations with her.
Do not have sexual relations with your brother's wife; that would dishonor your brother.
Do not have sexual relations with both a woman and her daughter. Do not have sexual relations with either her son's daughter or her daughter's daughter; they are her close relatives. That is wickedness."
Do not take your wife's sister as a rival wife and have sexual relations with her while your wife is living (Leviticus 18:6-18).

There is a common consequence that is repeated throughout these instructions, and that is <u>dishonor</u>. When a person engages in sexual activity with another family member that person dishonors and disgraces the entire family and themselves. Disgrace and dishonor have no part in God's design for intimacy. If you are struggling in this area, pray for the grace of God to be your strength and then see what you need to radically amputate in order to enjoy God-blessed intimacy in the future.

The last two perversions of sexual intimacy we will look at in this lesson are rape and prostitution. Rape is sexual activity against another person's will, and prostitution is sexual activity in exchange for something in return, usually money. Both are driven by lust and not by love. Sexual relations were never meant to be forced on another person, nor are they meant to be sold as merchandise. These perversions perform the act of sex, but are <u>totally void</u> of God-created riches of intimacy. They are illusions of satisfaction and not even close to the complete love and intimacy God has designed for us to enjoy. Having sex does not automatically mean intimacy. Don't sacrifice the wonders of intimacy for immediate gratification of a sexual desire. The gratification will not last and it is an illusion that will destroy you.

Question 8. Are there any thoughts, desires or actions that need to be radically amputated for you?

This is not light stuff we've discussed today! In the next few days, we will be taking a deeper look at the other perversions, namely pornography, self-gratification, adultery, fornication and homosexuality. None of it can be taken lightly, but are definitely real things that must be dealt with and guarded against for purity.

I waited patiently for the Lord; he turned to me and heard my cry. He lifted me out of the slimy pit, out of the mud and mire; he set my feet on a rock and gave me a firm place to stand. He put a new song in my mouth, a hymn of praise to our God. Many will see and fear and put their trust in the Lord. Blessed is the man who makes the Lord his trust, who does not look to the proud, to those who turn aside to false gods. Many, O Lord my God, are the wonders you have done. The things you planned for us no one can recount to you; were I to speak and tell of them, they would be too many to declare (Psalm 40:1-5).

Did you live sexually pure today?
        Yes   No

Are you committed to staying sexually pure?
        Yes   No

DAY 22
Nakedness

Just as sexuality was first created in the Garden of Eden, sexual sin and impurity also happened first in the Garden. Satan slipped into the Garden in the form of a serpent, and tempted Eve to eat the fruit God commanded them not to eat. Satan deceived Eve into thinking that God was not being truthful with them; that they would not die but become more like God. Once Eve ate from the fruit, Satan used her to get Adam also to eat from the fruit.

This act of rebellion separated man from God. The pure relationship that Adam and Eve once had with God was now broken. Because sin entered the world, all of mankind is born with the desire to sin and to rebel against God.

Let us look at something that took place in the Garden of Eden that symbolizes this fall. After God created Eve from Adam, and before they sinned, we read in Genesis 2:25 that, "the man and his wife were both naked, and they felt no shame." Reality! No hiding, no cover. Adam and Eve had no concept of nakedness, so they were not ashamed about being naked! It was the reality of how God had made them – wonderfully.

When the woman saw that the fruit of the tree was good for food and pleasing to the eye, and also desirable for gaining wisdom, she took some and ate it. She also gave some to her husband, who was with her, and he ate it. Then the eyes of both of them were opened, and they realized they were naked; so they sewed fig leaves together and made coverings for themselves.

Then the man and his wife heard the sound of the LORD God as he was walking in the garden in the cool of the day, and they hid from the LORD God among the trees of the garden. But the LORD God called to the man, "Where are you?" He answered, "I heard you in the garden, and I was afraid because I was naked; so I hid." And he said, "Who told you that you were naked? Have you eaten from the tree that I commanded you not to eat from? (Genesis 3:6-11).

In Genesis 3:7-11, we see that once they ate of the forbidden fruit, their eyes were opened. They realized they were naked and became ashamed. Adam and Eve hid themselves from God and from each other. Nakedness was now shameful. The beauty of God's utmost creation could no longer be openly displayed, but had to be hidden under clothes.

Because nakedness is so directly related to mankind's fall into sin, it is not surprising that it is the driving force behind sexual sin. Nakedness inside marriage is good and right, and we are designed to enjoy the reality of nakedness with our mates. However, outside of marriage, nakedness appeals to our sinful flesh. It tantalizes and excites us, and triggers thoughts of lust, fantasy and illusion. The pornography industry is based on the thrill of nakedness.

Now, it is important to understand that nakedness in its proper place is not sinful. It is the reality of who we are, created by God. It's good. The only time nakedness is to be shared is between a husband and a wife. Remember, in a marriage, two become one and a husband and wife know each other in ways no other person should know them. In the proper context, nakedness is part of the riches that God has designed for us in marriage! But used prematurely, before marriage, it hinders the richness of the marriage bed later. Our nakedness is to be guarded and protected, and not carelessly flaunted.

Let's review with some questions about what has been discussed so far in today's lesson.

Question 1. Originally, after God first created them, how did Adam and Eve feel about their nakedness according to Genesis 2:25 above?

Question 2. Satan deceived Adam and Eve into eating the forbidden fruit and they became aware of good and evil. How did they feel about their nakedness then?

Question 3. Explain in your own words the connection between nakedness and sin, especially sexual sin.

Question 4. What are we to do with our nakedness?

    A. Guard it and protect it

    B. Carelessly flaunt it

Also, the women are to dress themselves in modest clothing, with decency and good sense; not with elaborate hairstyles, gold, pearls, or expensive apparel, but with good works, as is proper for women who affirm that they worship God (1 Timothy 2:9-10 HCSB).

Question 5. How are women to dress themselves in order to show others that they worship God?

Question 6. According to God's standards, in what relationship and only with whom should one's nakedness be shared?

Perversion of Sexuality

Since God created nakedness as a wonderful thing, Satan naturally tries to destroy what God has designed as good. Today we will briefly touch on one perversion of God's wonderful design. This perversion is homosexuality. In the light of God's Word, there is no debate on homosexuality. It is a sin, and many are being led into an enslaving lifestyle in this sin. The clearest example of God's attitude toward homosexuality in particular, as well as sexual perversion in general, is to look at Sodom and Gomorrah. In the following Scriptures we see the perverseness of the people there.

Before they had gone to bed, all the men from every part of the city of Sodom— both young and old—surrounded the house. They called to Lot, "Where are the men who came to you tonight? Bring them out to us so that we can have sex with them.

Lot went outside to meet them and shut the door behind him and said, "No, my friends. Don't do this wicked thing. Look, I have two daughters who have never slept with a man. Let me bring them out to you, and you can do what you like with them. But don't do anything to these men, for they have come under the protection of my roof."

"Get out of our way," they replied. And they said, "This fellow came here as an alien, and now he wants to play the judge! We'll treat you worse than them." They kept bringing pressure on Lot and moved forward to break down the door. But the men inside reached out and pulled Lot back into the house and shut the door. Then they struck the men who were at the door of the house, young and old, with blindness so that they could not find the door.
The two men said to Lot, "Do you have anyone else here—sons-in-law, sons or daughters, or anyone else in the city who belongs to you? Get them out of here, because we are going to destroy this place. The outcry to the LORD against its people is so great that he has sent us to destroy it" (Genesis 19:4-13).

Question 7. According to the verses above, what did all the men want to do with Lot's guests?

Question 8. What were Lot's guests sent to do to Sodom and Gomorrah?

Then the Lord rained down burning sulfur on Sodom and Gomorrah – from the Lord out of the heavens (Genesis19:24).

Question 9. What happened to Sodom and Gomorrah?
    A. They had an interstate built over them
    B. The first Super Wal-Mart was built there
    C. They received the punishment of eternal burning fire
    D. They were passed up for the Olympics

If a man lies with a man as one lies with a woman, both of them have done what is detestable. They must be put to death; their blood will be on their own heads (Leviticus 20:13).

Question 10. What does God say here about homosexuality?

Do not lie with a man as one lies with a woman; that is detestable (Leviticus 18:22).

Question 11. What does God say here about homosexuality?

Because of this, God gave them over to shameful lusts. Even their women exchanged natural relations for unnatural ones. In the same way the men also abandoned natural relations with women and were inflamed with lust for one another. Men committed indecent acts with other men, and received in themselves the due penalty for their perversion.

Furthermore, since they did not think it worthwhile to retain the knowledge of God, he gave them over to a depraved mind, to do what ought not to be done. They have become filled with every kind of wickedness, evil, greed and depravity. They are full of envy, murder, strife, deceit and malice. They are gossips, slanderers, God-haters, insolent, arrogant and boastful; they invent ways of doing evil; they disobey their parents; they are senseless, faithless, heartless, ruthless. Although they know God's righteous decree that those who do such things deserve death, they not only continue to do these very things but also approve of those who practice them (Romans 1:26-32).

Question 12. According to these verses, what happened to those practicing homosexuality?

When you take a good hard look at our society, you will find there is not much separating us from Sodom and Gomorrah. We can't flip through the TV stations in the evening without running into pictures or humor about homosexuality.

131

Most likely there are kids in your high school who have already openly embraced a homosexual lifestyle. Even some churches seem to be struggling with their position on this issue. But do not allow yourself to be deceived! To entertain thoughts that we were not made to live according to God's standards, or that you were born with homosexual tendencies, is to listen to a lie from the Evil One. Of course, the Evil One wants to destroy you and he will offer any illusion, any explanation that will keep you from living as God created you to live. For some people, that temptation is homosexuality. But as with all other sexual sins, we must flee those things and people who tempt us to a lifestyle contrary to God's standards.

We must radically amputate anything that tempts us to sin against God. Eternity is on the line. You are playing with fire if you do not run full speed away from whatever sin entices you. No matter how careful you are, you will always get burned! If you are male, then God created you to live and function as a male; and if you are a female then God created you to live and function as a female. He has a grand purpose in mind for you. Please seek Him on this issue of homosexuality and don't be fooled into embracing a lie instead of the truth.

One other thought concerning homosexuality... if you struggle in this area at all, please talk to someone you trust who is godly, who will help show you God's forgiveness toward you in this issue and give you hope. Discover the victory at the end of the following passage:

Do you not know that the wicked will not inherit the kingdom of God? Do not be deceived: Neither the sexually immoral nor idolaters nor adulterers nor male prostitutes nor homosexual offenders, no thieves, not the greedy nor drunkards nor slanderers nor swindlers will inherit the kingdom of God. And this is what some of you were. But you were washed, you were sanctified, you were justified in the name of the Lord Jesus Christ, and by the Spirit of our God (1 Corinthians 6:9-11).

Notice Paul wrote, "such *were* some of you." Savor the knowledge that you can put off sinful habits and put on the righteousness of God through the Holy Spirit. Your parents are probably the best people to talk with about this subject. Or if you have a youth pastor or pastor, they can help too. Please don't try to sort through questions and struggles by yourself. There is always safety in numbers, and God will use the wise counsel of those around you who love you to keep you from the destruction that is connected to homosexuality. Also, we highly recommend the "Door of Hope" course at Setting Captives Free, which has freed hundreds and even thousands of people from homosexuality.

Despite all the perversions we've talked through yesterday and today, there is hope! Read this Scripture and enjoy the hope and promise written to you today!

You see, at just the right time, when we were still powerless, Christ died for the ungodly. Very rarely will anyone die for a righteous man, though for a good man someone might possibly dare to die. But God demonstrates his own love for us in this: While we were still sinners, Christ died for us.

Since we have now been justified by his blood, how much more shall we be saved from God's wrath through him! For if, when we were God's enemies, we were reconciled to him through the death of his Son, how much more, having been reconciled, shall we be saved through his life! Not only is this so, but we also rejoice in God through our Lord Jesus Christ, through whom we have now received reconciliation...

For if, by the trespass of the one man, death reigned through that one man, how much more will those who receive God's abundant provision of grace and of the gift of righteousness reign in life through the one man, Jesus Christ... For just as through the disobedience of the one man the many were made sinners, so also through the obedience of the one man the many will be made righteous (Romans 5:6-11, 13, 17, 19).

Did you live sexually pure today?
        Yes   *No*
Are you committed to staying sexually pure?
        Yes   *No*

Notes

DAY 23
Selling Short

The pastor stood in front of the crowd of smiling faces. With a wide grin of his own, he took a deep breath and announced, "It is my privilege to introduce to you for the first time, Mr. and Mrs. Nathan Wells. Nathan, you may kiss your bride." To many claps and a few hearty "Amens", Nathan leaned down and tenderly kissed his new bride. They were finally married! The cheering of their hearts was louder than that of any person in the crowd. They had waited so long for this day. The struggle for their own purity and to lead others in purity was an intense battle, but the Lord fought with them and protected them for this day. In a few more hours they would be off to Cancun for a week alone together. The connection this bride and groom shared was deep and in just a few more hours it was to become the deepest kind of connection God intended for a husband and wife. What joy they felt in becoming "one" together, with God cheering them on! Oh, how they wished everyone could experience the excitement, peace and strength of it all.

Two people becoming one. This is easy to understand sexually, but gets harder when we try to understand it mentally, emotionally, and spiritually. There is something very tangible or concrete when two people become one sexually, but not as tangible when they become one mentally, emotionally and spiritually. No matter how we say it, there is mystery, thrill and anticipation in becoming one with another person. This is good. It is God's design!

Fornication

There is something that perverts God's design of two people becoming one. It is pre-marital sexual activity or fornication. Simply put, fornication is sexual activity before marriage.

Question 1. What are your thoughts on pre-marital sex?

God loves two people becoming one. He created sex and He said it was good! Song of Solomon talks very erotically about sexual activity and the joy two lovers are meant to have in becoming one. But that oneness is only meant for marriage. God deals harshly with those who become one flesh outside of marriage. In contrast to today's society, it is interesting to look at what the Old Testament says about pre-marital sex:

If a man seduces a virgin who is not pledged to be married and sleeps with her, he must pay the bride-price, and she shall be his wife. If her father absolutely refuses to give her to him, he must still pay the bride-price for virgins (Exodus 22:16, 17).

Here is God's instruction to His people, that if a man sleeps with a virgin and has sexual relations with her, the man must make this woman his wife. The two people had become one, and so God commands them to live as one in marriage. Only the father has the authority to negate this arrangement, but the man must still pay the penalty for the loss of the woman's virginity.

Question 2. What are some ways you might have to pay a penalty for pre-marital sex?

Don't listen to the lie of the Evil One who tells you that you don't need to wait to have sex. Waiting for God's design is right and good. The pain and trouble caused by pre-marital sex far outweighs its very temporary pleasure. There is much joy in holding out, so don't sell yourself short by giving in to sex before you're committed in marriage.

Adultery

Adultery is closely related to fornication because it involves sexual relations between a man and a woman outside of marriage. But the critical difference in adultery is that at least one of them is already married to someone else. Of all the forms of sexual perversion, adultery is the only one mentioned in the Ten Commandments!

You shall not commit adultery (Exodus 20:14, Deuteronomy 5:18).

What is it about adultery that sets it apart from other sexual perversions? Why has adultery been singled out among all other sexual impurity? The answer is that in adultery, we see the greatest perversion of the mystery and blessing of sexuality – two people becoming one. Adultery destroys a commitment made to another before God. Adultery breaks the intimate bonds God has given to those in a marriage relationship. Through sexuality, two separate distinct humans become one flesh. This unity is to be forged in the lifelong covenant of marriage. When one of the partners steps outside of this covenant, they are breaking the promises of it. When he or she decides to have sexual relations with another person, then that person is joined with someone outside the original covenant. In a sense, the one flesh has died, because part of it is no longer there. It has joined itself with someone else.

Let's look at the penalty God gives for adultery:

If a man commits adultery with another man's wife—with the wife of his neighbor—both the adulterer and the adulteress must be put to death (Leviticus 20:10).

We see here God is not kidding around! A relationship—the sacred one-flesh union of man and woman—is being killed when one of the partners commits adultery. And because of this, the price to pay for adultery is extremely high. Now, today our society does not kill adulterers. But the above passages show the heart of God on the matter of adultery. God hates it and God hates all sexual impurity. It is wise for you to pray that God would make you a man or woman after His own heart, and that you too would come to detest adultery. Know that adultery destroys.

Question 3. What are your thoughts on adultery?

Some of you come from homes torn apart by adultery. Dad and Mom may be divorced because one or both of them committed adultery. The pain of adultery has a rippling effect, much like when you throw a stone into the water. At the moment of impact it begins to spread until the whole lake is experiencing the repercussions of one stone. Never let anyone tell you that one person's sin doesn't affect anyone else. Don't fall for the, "It's my life and my choice" mentality, believing that your actions only affect you.

God can bring restoration to your parents if they have committed adultery, even if they have remarried others. Oh, they may not be able to live together again, but if there is forgiveness requested and granted they can be friends, and God's grace can cover over their sin. Regardless of your parent's relationship, God will give you grace to endure. God can also give you the grace not to be involved in what your parents may have been. So even though God hates adultery, He gives grace to anyone who comes to Him in humility and repentance.

Purity Challenge member Jackie writes: My parents have been divorced since I was one. My mother's boyfriend was a very bad person, and did terrible things to my mom, my sister and me. When I finally said something about it, my mother called the police. However, she ended up marrying him. Over the last few years, my step-dad has been very verbally abusive. I can never explain to you the depth of pain that he caused me. But I can tell you how God has had mercy on me. I always loved going to church, and even when I was young I could understand that I needed Jesus, and that He was my Savior. I later got involved with a youth group and loved it. I believe I truly gave my life to Christ the summer before eighth grade. (This was after I started to mess around with sexual impurity.) I read romance novels and then because I wanted to know how the lovers felt, I would lust. I was in a Bible study and I still am. My accountability partner is my Bible study leader, who taught me about purity from day one.

Although I have grown as a Christian, I have been crippled in a large way because of lust. I had no self-control when it came to experimenting sexually because I did not know about the freedom I had in Christ! Now through this Purity Challenge course, I have been freed from sexual impurity for over a year—Praise God! I am praying that you too will find the courage and the humility to give up what is stopping you from finding true life in Christ. Whether you know it or not, any kind of sexual impurity is going to rot inside you until Christ sets you are free from the dominion of darkness. Christ loves you very much even though He knows everything about you. I pray that you are touched by this testimony.

Question 4. Maybe you've had a similar situation or know someone who has. As you think about the far-reaching pain adultery causes, what is going to stop you from doing the same thing when you are married?

As a child of a King, you have been created by and for the King and for the person He's planned for you to marry. To have pre-marital sex now, or commit adultery later is to cause great pain to the King and your future mate. To have pre-marital sex now or commit adultery later is to sell yourself short of God's amazing riches made just for you in the oneness of marriage.

Scripture for Today

"...For I know the plans I have for you," declares the LORD, "plans to prosper you and not to harm you, plans to give you hope and a future. Then you will call upon me and come and pray to me, and I will listen to you. You will seek me and find me when you seek me with all your heart. I will be found by you," declares the LORD, "and will bring you back from captivity" (Jeremiah 29:11-14).

Did you live sexually pure today?
      Yes   *No*

Are you committed to staying sexually pure?
      Yes   *No*

Notes

DAY 24
Temporary Illusion

For all that is in the world—the lust of the flesh, the lust of the eyes, and the pride of life—is not of the Father but is of the world" (1 John 2:16).

We will be wrapping up our discussion on sexual perversions in today and tomorrow's lessons by talking about two other major perversions that are diabolically linked together – pornography and self-gratification. (Self-gratification is better known as masturbation, but we prefer to use the more biblical term.) The demonic forces behind pornography and self-gratification have locked hundreds of thousands of souls in bondage. It is a definite challenge to society to seek purity in these areas.

Pornography

What is it about pornography and self-gratification that is so enslaving, perhaps more so than any other sexual sin we have discussed (except possibly homosexuality)? To understand this, we have to take a look at this beast and how powerful it is. First, let's start with some definitions to set a foundation.

The following are taken from Merriam-Webster's Dictionary:

> **pornography**: 1. the depiction of erotic behavior (as in pictures or writing) intended to cause sexual excitement 2: material (as books or a photograph) that depicts erotic behavior and is intended to cause sexual excitement 3. the depiction of acts in a sensational manner so as to arouse a quick intense emotional reaction.[22]

> **erotic**: 1. of, devoted to, or tending to arouse sexual love or desire <*erotic* art>
> 2. strongly marked or affected by sexual desire [23]

Question 1. What type of behavior does pornography capture and depict?

Question 2. What is the intended outcome/response of pornography?

The sole purpose of pornography is to spark sexual excitement and an intense emotional reaction. The two of these together is what makes pornography so addictive. There is a thrill behind each piece of pornography that captivates the viewer or reader causing him or her to seek out the next source of this pleasure. This is all driven by lust, which we talked about earlier in the course.

Question 3. Read again the Scripture written at the very beginning of this day. How does pornography line up with being "lust of the eyes and lust of the flesh"?

Question 4. According to 1 John 2:16 written above, if pornography is "lust of the flesh and lust of the eyes", then pornography is...
   A. of God
   B. of the world
   C. of a galaxy far, far away

The billion dollar pornography industry is one of the few businesses that thrives and succeeds by customer dissatisfaction. This is important to understand. Because of the thrill and pleasure pornography provides, and the hunger and wanting for more it creates, it leaves those who use pornography in an endless cycle of not being satisfied. They may feel satisfied in that moment of intense emotional reaction, but once it is over, the person is left empty and most often feeling worse for having just used pornography. Therefore, pornography is similar to an alcohol or drug addiction because the more you have, the more you want.

Pornography is not only an illusion, but temporary at that. Consider this story:

> *A man is walking through the desert. He thought he brought enough water to make it across the desert in the three days it was supposed to take him to reach his destination. Three days into the journey he drank his last drop of water, yet his destination was nowhere in sight. Out of water and uncertain how to reach his destination, he continued walking. It wasn't long before he thought he saw something up ahead. He blinked his eyes and wiped the sweat from his brow and looked again. Sure enough, he thought, "That's a small pond up ahead with shade trees surrounding it." So the man mustered all the strength he had left, ran to the bank of the pond and jumped in – face first! When he came up he had a mouth full of sand and was even thirstier than before.*

This is what happens to thousands of people everyday! They set out on the journey of life, only to be drained of their resources through discouragement, failure and sin. And then, instead of going to the only One who can refuel them, they run to the desert oasis called pornography and once there end up thirstier than ever.

Do not be deceived! Pornography can take on many forms, and the less obvious forms of pornography can gradually lead a person into deeper forms, making it harder to break free. The soft porn of certain magazines like Playboy and Penthouse often leads to more graphic and explicit forms of porn. Even romance novels and soap operas can be subtle sources of porn that can easily be overlooked. Often it only takes a commercial that shows skin or two people touching each other to spark the fire of lust.

Do not be deceived! There are many that say this is a victimless, harmless pastime—not true! Pornography does not care about age, racial background, income level, or anything like that. Men and women, young and old, rich and poor, and everyone down the line can be taken in by this diabolical force. It is an equal-opportunity destroyer! It is not something to play with or toy with, because while it only takes a moment to fall into its grip, it can take a lifetime to break free. Its captives are men and women who lose time and money, family and jobs, and sometimes their lives. Its victims are the spouses of those who are addicted to porn because they often feel they have lost the love and affection of their partners. Even worse are the consequences when use of porn is exposed to public scrutiny in the workplace, schools and churches. It is demeaning to the women and girls who expose themselves for the lustful delight and pleasure of men. These women who are wives, mothers, daughters, and sisters are reduced to a fake, touched-up, painted image on print.

Pornography is Idolatry

If you have been exposed to pornography, either directly or indirectly by someone else, it is important to break the chains now. It is important to see that pornography is idolatry. "How so?" you may ask. Well, it drives people to find a source of pleasure and satisfaction that is not in God, or in the marital relationship that God designed for sexual pleasure and satisfaction. Therefore, as stated earlier, it is a false sort of satisfaction. Any satisfaction that is not found in God's design and for His glory is an idol. Anything worshiped and pursued above God is an idol.

Also, in the days of the Old Testament, it was common practice to set an altar of worship on a high hill or mountain. The idea behind this was to get close to God. When Israel turned from God and allowed the nations around them to build their altars to the false gods they served, God commanded His people to tear down the high places.

Similarly, pornography makes its way into the "high places" of our minds. It is at the forefront of one's thoughts and becomes the only thing someone thinks about. In that regard, pornography comes between God and that individual. As that person is driven to seek new sources of pornography, he or she is no longer a servant to God, but a slave to porn because it becomes the controlling force in a mind and life.

Question 5. Do you see how pornography is a form of idolatry?

Question 6. Explain this principle in your own words.

God wants you to serve Him fully. He does not want you to be a slave to anything, but to be a willing bondservant to Him. Jesus came, died on the cross, and rose from death to set us all free from sin. Therefore we are not to place ourselves in any form of sinful bondage. The question now is, are you willing to avoid any and all forms of pornography as best as you are able?

Getting Out of Its Grip

If you have become exposed to pornography in some way, it is not too late for you to break the chains and step out of its grip before it tightens around you. This is not to condemn you, but to hopefully bring about godly conviction over pornography usage. The next step in cutting loose is confession and the final step is repentance.

Conviction is feeling sorrow because you've sinned against God. This is a positive thing, as God is speaking to your heart and desiring you to turn away from sin and back to Him.

Confession is the way you respond to conviction. It is admitting you have sinned and communicating directly to God about your sin, not hiding anything.

Repentance is to completely turn away from sin and begin walking the opposite way toward God, leaving previous sin and all of its "relatives" behind.

...do you show contempt for the riches of his kindness, tolerance and patience, not realizing that God's kindness leads you toward repentance? (Romans 2:4).

But because of your stubbornness and your unrepentant heart, you are storing up wrath against yourself for the day of God's wrath, when his righteous judgment will be revealed (Romans 2:5).

Question 7. According to Romans 2:4 above, what leads us to repentance?

Question 8. According to Romans 2:5 above, to disobey and ignore God's kindness leads to what?

If there is sin in your life about which you are convicted, don't miss the great opportunity to talk to God about it. Below, write out a prayer of confession to God asking for His forgiveness and grace to cover over your sin completely. Also, ask him to help you turn away from the sin and walk whole-heartedly toward Him.

Question 9. Please write your confession, prayers and thoughts here.

Dean, age 14, writes: I had struggled with soft porn since I was about 10. I really didn't think there was anything wrong with it until I came to this website and found this course. By the grace of God I have radically amputated the sin in my life. It will only be because of God's help that I will stay pure.

You can break free from sexual sin. No matter if it is a few impure thoughts every now and then or if you are deeply involved in pornography and self-gratification. Ask God today to give you His grace to turn away from all sexual sin and follow Christ!

Scripture to Consider

For though we live in the world, we do not wage war as the world does. The weapons we fight with are not the weapons of the world. On the contrary, they have divine power to demolish strongholds. We demolish arguments and every pretension that sets itself up against the knowledge of God, and we take captive every thought to make it obedient to Christ (2 Corinthians 10:3-5).

Did you live sexually pure today?
     Yes   *No*

Are you committed to staying sexually pure?
     Yes   *No*

DAY 25
Scooping Fire in Your Lap

Can a man scoop fire into his lap without his clothes being burned? (Proverbs 6:27).

It's like petting a wild animal... You may think it's okay and harmless, but it awakens a raging animal that will devour you before you even realize it.

We continue our study of sexual purity today by taking a look at what is commonly called masturbation. For this study, we will use the more biblical term of self-gratification. As a teen and young adult, chances are the majority of time when self-gratification comes up in discussion it is in a joking manner. However, there is nothing funny about gratification of the flesh. It is a serious subject, as it is an activity that can become very addicting. In many ways, self-gratification is the other side of the same coin as pornography. They wickedly fuel each other and mercilessly feed off each other, driving the one in bondage to them deeper into a bottomless pit from which there can seem to be little hope of escape.

> **A Course Member writes:** When I lived with my parents during High School, I would wait for them to go to bed and I would stay up later. I would lie on the couch for sometimes 3 hours or more channel-surfing the TV, looking for just the right piece of flesh with which to gratify myself. Of course, the volume was always low enough so I could hear if my parents were coming back downstairs and I could switch channels quickly. I wasted many hours and was totally controlled by lust in those moments.

In the Bible there are no Scriptures that speak on this subject directly. You will not find the term 'masturbation' in the Bible. If this is so, then how can self-gratification be wrong? That's a good question, and the answer is that even though there is nothing specifically on masturbation, there are many Scriptures that can give us direction and insight on where this fits in God's plan.

This lesson will be a little different from the others. Today, we will give you seven Scriptures and ask that you give your insights and thoughts on them. Keep these questions in mind as you read and then comment on each Scripture:
1. How does self-gratification fit in this verse?
2. If this verse were speaking specifically on self-gratification, what would it be saying about it?
3. In light of this verse, would self-gratification be okay or not?

Before going on, there is one important comment that needs to be made. If you are someone who has experimented with self-gratification, this lesson – like yesterday's lesson on pornography – is not here to condemn you. May this lesson clearly show you the true reality about self-gratification, and what God wants for you and your life.

But among you there must not be even a hint of sexual immorality, or of any kind of impurity, or of greed, because these are improper for God's holy people (Ephesians 5:3).

Question 1. Use the above three questions regarding self-gratification, and write your thoughts here.

Flee from sexual immorality. All other sins a man commits are outside his body, but he who sins sexually sins against his own body. Do you not know that your body is a temple of the Holy Spirit, who is in you, whom you have received from God? You are not your own; you were bought at a price. Therefore honor God with your body (1 Corinthians 6:18-20).

Question 2. Write your thoughts here concerning self-gratification and this verse.

Don't you know that you yourselves are God's temple and that God's Spirit lives in you? (1 Corinthians 3:16).
Question 3. What are your thoughts and feelings about this truth?

So I say, live by the Spirit, and you will not gratify the desires of the sinful nature. For the sinful nature desires what is contrary to the Spirit, and the Spirit what is contrary to the sinful nature. They are in conflict with each other, so that you do not do what you want (Galatians 5:16-18).

Question 4. Living by the Spirit keeps us from doing what?

Those who live according to the sinful nature have their minds set on what that nature desires; but those who live in accordance with the Spirit have their minds set on what the Spirit desires. The mind of sinful man is death, but the mind controlled by the Spirit is life and peace; the sinful mind is hostile to God. It does not submit to God's law, nor can it do so. Those controlled by the sinful nature cannot please God (Romans 8:5-8).

Question 5. In light of this verse, would self-gratification be okay or not?

In a large house there are articles not only of gold and silver, but also of wood and clay; some are for noble purposes and some for ignoble. If a man cleanses himself from the latter, he will be an instrument for noble purposes, made holy, useful to the Master and prepared to do any good work. Flee the evil desires of youth, and pursue righteousness, faith, love and peace, along with those who call on the Lord out of a pure heart (2 Timothy 2:20-22).

Question 6. Cleansing yourself from things that are not noble (that are wrong), will make you what?

Flee what?

Pursue what?

After considering these Scriptures, we hope that you have come to realize the following critical points:
- Our body is a temple of God's Spirit; self-gratification serves the flesh and lust.
- We are God's vessel, to be used for His purposes; self-gratification is the opposite of God's purpose for sex
- Our bodies are to be instruments of righteousness; self-gratification leads to bondage to sin

Question 7. What are your final thoughts and comments or questions on self-gratification?

In closing, we would like for you to read this testimony. It is the typical story. Pornography and self-gratification are always linked.

> **Course member Chris writes:** I am currently 19 years old and I first gratified myself only a few months ago. When I first did it, I thought "Oh no, this is so wrong, I'll never do it again." But a week later I did it again, and that's where my addiction started. At first it was just action, but eventually impure thoughts started going with that action. I became so hooked to the habit that I was doing it about four times a day. It didn't stop there. I discovered pornography in my house accidentally (it didn't belong to me). I became addicted to porn as well and began gratifying myself and using porn regularly. Throughout the time, I recognize that God was trying to steer me back onto the right path. He provided people for me to talk to and of course, Purity Challenge! Thank God!

If you would like more information on the subject of self-gratification and how to be free from it, simply send a blank email to masturbation@settingcaptivesfree.com and we will send you an article that was written by the Setting Captives Free staff.

Scripture to Consider

Therefore do not let sin reign in your mortal body so that you obey its evil desires. Do not offer the parts of your body to sin, as instruments of wickedness, but rather offer yourselves to God, as those who have been brought from death to life; and offer the parts of your body to him as instruments of righteousness. For sin shall not be your master, because you are not under law, but under grace. What then? Shall we sin because we are not under law but under grace? By no means! Don't you know that when you offer yourselves to someone to obey him as slaves, you are slaves to the one whom you obey--whether you are slaves to sin, which leads to death, or to obedience, which leads to righteousness? (Romans 6:12–16).

Did you live sexually pure today?
  Yes   No

Are you committed to staying sexually pure?
  Yes   No

DAY 26
Know the Battle

Gird your sword upon your side, O mighty one; clothe yourself with splendor and majesty (Psalm 45:3).

Make no mistake; you are in a battle. To think otherwise is certain defeat. During the next two days, we will examine the tactics of the enemy of our souls. We will also help you develop some battle strategies of your own to combat him. Please read the following verses, paying close attention to exactly where the enemy wages war on us.

For though we live in the world, we do not wage war as the world does. The weapons we fight with are not the weapons of the world. On the contrary, they have divine power to demolish strongholds. We demolish arguments and every pretension that sets itself up against the knowledge of God, and we take captive every thought to make it obedient to Christ (2 Corinthians 10:3-5).

Question 1. From the above verses, <u>where</u> does the Devil attack us? In other words, where is the battle fought?
    A. In Battleground, Washington
    B. In political and cultural issues
    C. In the mind; in our thoughts

Question 2. <u>What</u> does the enemy attack?
    A. Our sense of humor
    B. Our pride
    C. Our knowledge of God

Question 3. What do the above verses call evil thoughts that can get lodged in our minds?
    A. Strongholds
    B. Brain teasers
    C. Common and ordinary thoughts

We are in a war and the battlefield is our mind. The enemy fights to set up thought "strongholds" in our minds in order to hold us captive to him. These are thoughts that won't go away, and he knows that we will eventually act upon them. These "strongholds" are whatever is opposed to "the knowledge of God." Here is how one student put it: *"I want to leave behind all forms of sexual impurity that pervade my life. First, the endless and repetitive pornographic thoughts I have throughout the day which leads into viewing pornography, mostly on the web, but occasionally with videos and magazines, and of course self-gratification."* Can you see where his thoughts are first captured and how they lead to further sin?

So let's think through a temptation scenario as it may really happen. Everything seems fine, and then all of a sudden a lustful picture comes into your thoughts. The image is lodged in your brain causing you to dwell on it. THIS is the beginning of a thought-stronghold. You are not thinking of God or anything worthwhile during this time, but of where the thought wants to lead you... not toward God, but as a chained captive away from God. See the reality of the temptation. The image that is lodged in your mind is in opposition to the knowledge of God. After all, the knowledge of God is whatever is true, noble, right, pure, lovely, and admirable (Philippians 4:8), and on such we are to constantly think. We can understand then that the evil one is setting that lustful image up in our minds to turn us away from God. This image, and the associated emotions conjured up in the heart, if not fought immediately, can become a stronghold of the Devil, and lead us into other sins.

Question 4. Describe a temptation scenario in your life and how it began in your mind.

We need to make sure we understand that our minds are a battleground. And most importantly, we need to possess "divine weapons" and know how to fight using them. Notice the following verses with our emphasis added:

The <u>mind</u> of sinful man is death... (Romans 8:6).

The sinful <u>mind</u> is hostile to God. It does not submit to God's law nor can it do so (Romans 8:7).

Many live as the enemies of the cross of Christ. Their destiny is destruction, their god is their stomach, and their glory is in their shame. Their <u>mind</u> is on earthly things (Philippians 3:19).

Furthermore, since they did not think it worthwhile to retain the knowledge of God, he gave them over to a depraved <u>mind</u>, to do what ought not to be done. They have become filled with every kind of wickedness, evil, greed and depravity. They are full of envy, murder, strife, deceit and malice (Romans 1:28-29).

But I see another law at work in the members of my body, waging war against the law of my <u>mind</u> and making me a prisoner of the law of sin at work within my members (Romans 7:23).

In the above verses, we see that the mind of sinful man is death. These verses also show us that the sinful mind is totally against God. The evil one tries to get us to focus our minds on "earthly things" (things right here in front of us instead of God and heavenly things) and when he is successful we are bound for destruction. In Romans 7:23 above, we see that the war is waged against the mind, and when the enemy is successful in capturing our minds, we become prisoners of sin.

Question 5. Personal reflection: Have you felt at times that you were unable to control your mind? What "strongholds" have you experienced in the past that prove your mind is a battlefield?

Tomorrow we will begin to learn the resources with which we may fight. Meanwhile, we need to be aware of where the main battlefield is—the thought life, and how the Devil gets access to our hearts—through our thoughts. Please be on guard. "Your enemy, the devil, prowls around like a roaring lion looking for someone to devour" (1 Peter 5:8). And one of the ways he "devours" is through these thought-strongholds.

Here are two things we can do to combat these thoughts that get lodged in our minds:

1. **RADICALLY AMPUTATE: We can refuse to have access to anything that could create impure images that could drag us into sin.** This point is important. To have victories in this area, we must allow NO access to anything that will give the Devil a foothold. Please see Matthew 5:29-30, Romans 13:14 and Joshua 7:13.
2. **RADICALLY CONSUME: We need to begin to soak ourselves in the Truth of Scripture, seeking God for grace to apply what we read.** Taking in the Word of God (The Living Water) has the effect of washing away the images that remain in the brain. Please check out Joshua 1:8 and Psalm 1:3.

As we, by the grace of God, continue to practice these two principles, we will become free from the strongholds of the enemy, and more like Jesus Christ.

Remember, this is not a one-time battle we are fighting. It is an *everyday*, moment-by-moment war from which we can never back down! Sound tiring? It is, and it always will be. The evil one knows that we do not possess the strength to continually fight the battle on our own. He will continue to attack and wear us down until we fail, unless we are fighting in the strength of our Lord Jesus Christ. Remember the promise of Romans 8:37: No, in all these things we are more than conquerors through him who loved us. In order to have that kind of endurance, and be *more* than a conqueror, set your mind on where your strength, focus and purity come from – the Conqueror himself, Jesus Christ. He has already won!

Question 6. Please record in your own words the two ideas referred to above, that will help rid the mind of lustful images:

1.

2.

> **Course Member Jim writes:** When we fight Satan, it is in our minds. By God's grace, we take down strongholds that he has put there. Satan does not want me to be free from porn, and is far from being done with me. However, God will help me because my purity is His will, I am sure of this. Satan will continue to attack. I would be a fool to think that Satan will just leave me alone. God has been mighty in my life recently, and this is just the beginning. All of this has happened in my mind, in the spiritual realm. It is a war, and we are in the midst of it all. I will not become a casualty of war. I will not become MIA or POW. I am going to pray that GOD will not let that happen. And, because I know that that is HIS Will, HE will do it. Best of all, we know who wins the war. GOD DOES!

Scripture to Consider

Romans 12:1-2 Therefore, I urge you, brothers, in view of God's mercy, to offer your bodies as living sacrifices, holy and pleasing to God-this is your spiritual act of worship. Do not conform any longer to the pattern of this world, but be transformed by the renewing of your mind. Then you will be able to test and approve what God's will is-his good, pleasing and perfect will.

Did you live sexually pure today?
     Yes   *No*

Are you committed to staying sexually pure?
     Yes   *No*

DAY 27
Battle Strategies, Part 1: Be Defensive!

To be victorious in any battle, you need to be strong in two areas: The offense and the defense. The offense is the force that seeks out the enemy and attacks in order to destroy the chance of an attack reoccurring. The defense is the force that defends, protects and guards the "home front", that which is valued and highly prized. Over the next two days we will discuss both offensive and defensive ways to pursue purity. Both are important and each will take strength and courage. First we will look at two of our best defensive tactics.

Defense Tactic #1: Break the Chain!

Headline: "Misloaded Douglas DC-8 Pitches Up Excessively On Takeoff, then Stalls and Strikes the Ground"

On this plane crash, the cargo was not loaded aboard the airplane according to the airlines instructions. As a result, the flight crew inadvertently used a setting that was not correct for the airplane's center of gravity. Here are the facts of what happened:

From the Flight Safety Foundation Editorial Staff:
"On August 7, 1997, (airline name) Flight 101, a Douglas DC-8-61, stalled on takeoff and struck the ground approximately 3,000 feet (915 meters) from the end of Runway 27R at Miami (Florida, U.S.) International Airport. The three flight crewmembers, a security guard aboard the airplane and one person on the ground (a motorist) were killed. The U.S. National Transportation Safety Board (NTSB), in its final report said the accident resulted from the airplane being misloaded to produce a more aft center of gravity and a correspondingly incorrect stabilizer-trim setting that precipitated an extreme pitch-up at rotation.

NTSB said that the probable causes of the accident were: The failure of (airline name) to exercise operational control over the cargo-loading process; [and,] The failure of [a freight-forwarding company] to load the airplane as specified by (airline name).

Contributing to the accident was the failure of the [U.S.] Federal Aviation Administration (FAA) to adequately monitor (airline name) operational-control responsibilities for cargo loading and the failure of FAA to ensure that known cargo-related deficiencies were corrected at (airline name), said NTSB.

The captain, 42, was hired by (airline name) in October 1993. He had 12,154 hours of flight time, including 2,522 hours as a (airline name) DC-8 captain. NTSB said that in 1995 the FAA suspended the captain's airman certificate and medical certificate for 30 days because he had failed to report a revocation of his motor-vehicle driver's license. FAA records indicated that the captain was convicted for misdemeanor drunk driving in California in 1986 and convicted for driving under the influence in Arizona in 1994, said NTSB."

As an airline pilot, I (Mike) often read up on the how's and why's of aircraft accidents. I do this to try to learn what happened and how I can prevent something similar from happening to me, the crew, and the passengers I carry. One of the greatest sites for studying aviation accidents is Flight Safety Foundation's Accident Prevention website at http://www.flightsafety.org/accident_prevention.html. One thing I have been noticing as I read through the accident reports is that there is usually an accident "chain" with many links that make up that chain. In the above accident what "links" in the accident chain can you find? Here are some that I saw:

1. Improper loading of the aircraft by the company contracted to load.
2. The airline did not properly monitor the loading of the aircraft.
3. Failure of the FAA to properly monitor the loading operation of the airline.
4. Failure of the FAA to ensure that previously known loading problems were corrected.
5. A possible fifth "link" in the accident chain could have been the captain's known drinking problem.

All the above links in the chain caused the accident of this Cargo Flight 101, killing a total of 5 people. What if just one link in the accident chain had been broken? For instance, what if the FAA, citing known loading problems with the airline, had decided to shut it down until its problems could be corrected? That one break in the chain would have saved five people's lives.

You and I may have had a problem with sin, including impure thoughts or actions. And if we examine times of failure we will always find a chain of events that leads up to the "crash." Here are some of mine:

1. I did not get up early and spend quiet time with the Lord.
2. I had a long day at work and I am tired.
3. My wife and I are at odds over something and we haven't talked often today, which means less accountability.
4. My last flight of the day was delayed because of weather and I had to stay overnight at a hotel.

5. I saw a partially clothed woman at the airport and I thought about her all day.
6. When I get to my hotel room I turn on the TV and immediately see an advertisement for a lustful movie I know I shouldn't watch.

Crash!

Now, I have learned to notice when links in an accident chain are developing and to break at least one link to prevent a sexual "accident", or dwelling on impure thoughts. So, now I rise early and spend time with the Lord, which sets me in a content and praying frame of mind throughout the day. I will communicate much with my wife, who is my accountability partner, and ensure we are loving to other. If my day is long, I know I'm headed for trouble and I begin watching and praying more intently for God's help. And finally, I might do something very practical to help break the chain, like take the TV out of my hotel room.

Next, let us notice how these "accident links" are all there in a particular incident in Scripture.

In the life of Lot, Abraham's nephew, there was a terrible tragedy. He came to live in a city that was ultimately destroyed by God for its wickedness. Lot lost all his possessions; his wife was killed and he barely escaped with his own life and the lives of his two daughters. Read the following passage of Scripture and see if you can spot the links in this developing "accident chain," then write in each "link" below.

So Abram said to Lot, "Let's not have any quarreling between you and me, or between your herdsmen and mine, for we are brothers. Is not the whole land before you? Let's part company. If you go to the left, I'll go to the right; if you go to the right, I'll go to the left."

Lot looked up and saw that the whole plain of the Jordan was well watered, like the garden of the LORD, like the land of Egypt, toward Zoar. (This was before the LORD destroyed Sodom and Gomorrah.) So Lot chose for himself the whole plain of the Jordan and set out toward the east. The two men parted company: Abram lived in the land of Canaan, while Lot lived among the cities of the plain and pitched his tents near Sodom. Now the men of Sodom were wicked and were sinning greatly against the LORD (Genesis 13:8-13).

The four kings seized all the goods of Sodom and Gomorrah and all their food; then they went away. They also carried off Abram's nephew Lot and his possessions, since he was living in Sodom (Genesis 14:11-12).

Question 1. List the "links" you can find that caused Lot's trouble (Lot and all his possessions being carried away by foreign kings). Here's the first one:

    1. First link: Lot and Abraham separated because of a quarrel.

    Now, see if you can find 3 or 4 more links and write them in here:

    2.

    3.

    4.

    5.

Now let's think of some ways to "break the chain" in Lot's story. These are some of the "links" in Lot's story:

1. **Lot and Abraham quarrel and separate** (13:8-11). What if Lot and Abraham had worked out their differences instead of separating? *Be careful not to separate yourselves from other believers and positive influences.*

2. **Lot "looked up and saw" the valley of Sodom** (13:10). What if Lot had not focused on the valley but on the hill country instead? *Be careful of your focus.*

3. **Lot "set out toward" Sodom** (13:11). Would this "accident" have happened if Lot had set out in another direction instead of Sodom? *Be careful of the general direction of your life. We are always moving, either more toward righteousness or more toward sin.*

4. **Lot "pitched his tent near" Sodom** (13:12). Lot could have broken the "accident chain" even after he separated from Abraham, and after he saw and set out toward Sodom, had he simply refused to pitch his tent so close to the filth and wretchedness of Sodom. *We still must influence the world, but we have to watch ourselves, be careful, and use wisdom and common sense as to how close we should "pitch our tent" in the world.*

5. **Lot "was living in" Sodom** (14:12). Notice the progression: Lot separated from Abraham, saw Sodom, set out toward Sodom, pitched his tent near Sodom, and ended up living in Sodom. And then we read of him being taken captive in battle. *These can be our steps to destruction and captivity as well. We separate from fellowship, see something sinful and focus on it, set out toward it, pitch our tent near it, live in it, and end up being taken captive by it.*

Now, let's follow a typical high school guy through his day as an example of the links that can lead to trouble. We'll name him Jack.

Jack watched Monday night football last night. The game was good, the cheerleaders were nice to look at, and the game ended late. Then he remembered he had a paper due the next day, so he had to stay up until 3 a.m. to finish. While he was doing some research on the internet he accidentally ran across some pictures that intrigued him. He was sick of research, so he took a few minutes to chat online with some girls. Of course when he finally went to sleep he missed his alarm the next morning and had to rush out the door to barely make it to school on time. Lately, he had been trying to spend a few minutes with God before he got to school, but this day he completely forgot in the rush. When he got to class, first period, his teacher yelled at him for something he didn't even do! So irritating! Back in the hallway after class, his girlfriend was talking to some guy at the locker next to hers. That made Jack mad. After school, Jack gave his girlfriend a ride home and told her how he didn't like her talking to other guys. His girlfriend, liking his jealous attention and wanting to reassure him, invited him into her house to talk through things, even though her parents weren't home. Jack went in and totally forgot about his plan to spend time with God after school, since he missed it that morning. Up in her bedroom, they sat on her bed and talked things out. In fact, they did so well at talking things out, they ended up making out and going farther than either of them had planned. **Crash!**

Question 2. What were some "links" in the chain that Jack could have changed that would probably have avoided the "crash" in the end?

Question 3. What chain of events has led you to impurity in the past?

Question 4. What links will you remove to avoid crashing into sin and how will you do it?

Question 5. Will you share this plan with someone who can help you implement it and hold you accountable for it?

Defense Tactic #2: Don't Go Near!

In July of 1972, a McDonnell Douglas DC-9, loaded with 85 passengers and 5 crewmembers, was traveling from St. Louis, Missouri, to Minneapolis, Minnesota. The time of departure was 2:30 pm and the aircraft had been airborne approximately 25 minutes. It was a typically hot and humid summer afternoon in the Midwest, with numerous thunderstorms building along the route of flight.

The Air Traffic Control monitor noticed the aircraft approaching the vicinity of several heavy thunderstorm buildups, and radioed this information: "(airline name) flight 2164, weather radar indicates you are approaching an area of level 5 buildups with tops above Flight Level 410. Suggest an Easterly deviation to heading 105 degrees within the next 10 miles."
The response from the pilots came back. "Uh, Roger, Kansas City Center, we see the thunderstorms. Onboard radar indicates a possible hole to penetrate through the buildups at our 12 O'clock position and 18 miles. Do you agree?"

Air Traffic Control replied, "Negative, flight 2164, our radar does not confirm the existence of a hole in the storm, suggest an easterly deviation to the right immediately."

"Uh, Roger, Kansas City Center, we will proceed straight ahead...it may be a little close, but we, uh, do see a hole to penetrate."

This was the last transmission recorded from this aircraft on Air Traffic Control's tapes. The aircraft penetrated the severest part of the storm, a level 5 thunderstorm, and was sent plummeting to the earth, killing all 91 people aboard. What happened?

Aircraft radar is susceptible to what is known as "attenuation" which is the blocking of any weather returns that are behind severe storms. Because there is so much moisture in severe thunderstorms, the radar is unable to penetrate through the moisture to be able to accurately present any weather information immediately behind the severe storms. In the above situation the radar, because of attenuation, falsely presented the appearance of a safe route of flight. Seasoned and well-trained pilots are aware of the problem of attenuation and know to remain well clear of all thunderstorms. The key to safety is to not go anywhere near a storm.

For us, impurity is a thunderstorm. But it can present the appearance of being harmless; a little fun, something that doesn't hurt anyone, a release for pent-up sexual energy. And yet impurity is a trap of the devil that has devastated the lives of countless people. How do we deal with this thunderstorm?

Answer: **Don't go near!**
Let's learn what the Bible says on the subject: Don't go near. Please read the following passage and answer the questions at the bottom. Can you discover the approaching "thunderstorm?"

At the window of my house I looked out through the lattice. I saw among the simple, I noticed among the young men, a <u>youth who lacked judgment.</u> He was going down the street near her corner, walking along in the direction of her house at twilight, as the day was fading, as the dark of night set in. Then out came a woman to meet him, dressed like a prostitute and with crafty intent. (She is loud and defiant, her feet never stay at home; now in the street, now in the squares, at every corner she lurks.) She took hold of him and kissed him and with a brazen face she said, "I have fellowship offerings at home; today I fulfilled my vows. So I came out to meet you; I looked for you and have found you! I have covered my bed with colored linens from Egypt. I have perfumed my bed with myrrh, aloes and cinnamon. Come, let's drink deep of love till morning; let's enjoy ourselves with love! My husband is not at home; he has gone on a long journey. He took his purse filled with money and will not be home till full moon."

With persuasive words she led him astray; <u>she seduced him with her smooth talk.</u> All at once he followed her like an ox going to the slaughter, like a deer stepping into a noose till an arrow pierces his liver, like a bird darting into a snare, little knowing it will cost him his life. Now then, my sons, listen to me; pay attention to what I say. Do not let your heart turn to her ways or stray into her paths. Many are the victims she has brought down; her slain are a mighty throng. <u>Her house is a highway to the grave</u>, leading down to the chambers of death" (Proverbs 7:6-27, emphasis added).

Question 6. In the passage above, the young man is doing something foolish. What is it?
   A. Going out at night without a coat
   B. Going near a prostitute's home, walking in her direction

Question 7. What words are used to describe this young man?
   A. Simple, lacking judgment
   B. Blond, well-muscled
   C. Able to go near temptation and say no to it

Here is something important to note: "All at once he followed her." Here is the problem with going "near" the temptation: the choice to sin is often made all of a sudden and without rational thought. If this young man were reasonable and rational, he could have weighed out the benefits versus the disadvantages. He could have said, "I will think about it and let you know," or he could have asked a friend for advice before acting. But powerful temptation removes one's ability to be rational and decisions are often made "all at once". The longer we stay involved in impurity the more things we do simply by impulse! Our best defense is avoidance at all costs!

Question 8. The passage above uses four analogies to describe what the end result of giving in to temptation is like. What are they? Here is the first one:

   Giving in to temptation is like:

   A. An Ox Going To The Slaughter

   B.

   C.

   D.

It helps to keep in mind what the final outcome of any sin will be. Sin inevitably leads to death. It may lead to physical death, or it may lead to death of your future marriage, or the death of your spiritual life, etc.

Question 9. The temptress promised an enjoyment of life. But according to the last couple of verses where did her paths actually lead?
   A. To the White House
   B. To the enjoyment of life
   C. To death and the grave

What could have been this young man's battle strategy against the death he was facing? You know the answer: **Don't go near!** Sometimes this is extremely difficult as temptation is "now in the street, now in the squares, at every corner she lurks." Remember the battle is everyday! Do everything possible to avoid temptation. Make a list of things you refuse to "go near". Here are some examples of practical lines you can draw to help you not go near temptation. Read these and then write your own list of boundaries below. You can include these examples in your own list if you want!

Don't Go Near: Boundaries I will make: (examples)
1. Refuse to be <u>alone</u> in a house with someone of the opposite sex.
2. Keep all clothing <u>on</u> when with your boyfriend or girlfriend
3. Don't surf the Internet after 10. pm.
4. Don't watch movies with known sexuality or nudity.

In the paths of the wicked lie thorns and snares, but he who guards his soul stays far from them (Proverbs 22:5).

Question 10. Write your list of defensive boundaries below that you will implement:

Question 11. What are the two defensive battle strategies discussed today?

1.

2.

Scripture for Today

Do not set foot on the path of the wicked or walk in the way of evil men. Avoid it, do not travel on it; turn from it and go on your way (Proverbs 4:14-15).

Avoid every kind of evil (1 Thessalonians 5:22).

Rather, clothe yourselves with the Lord Jesus Christ, and do not think about how to gratify the desires of the sinful nature (Romans 13:14).

For everything that was written in the past was written to teach us, so that through endurance and the encouragement of the Scriptures we might have hope (Romans 15:4).

Did you live sexually pure today?
     Yes   *No*

Are you committed to staying sexually pure?
     Yes   No

DAY 28
Battle Strategies, Part 2: Get Offensive!

"Enemy-occupied territory—that is what this world is."
C.S. Lewis

Earlier, we discussed the location of this enemy territory. We learned that our minds are the main battleground in which a war is being waged for our souls. Remember the verse from two days ago: "But I see another law at work in the members of my body, waging war against the law of my mind and making me a prisoner of the law of sin at work within my members" (Romans 7:23).

It is important to know that there is good news concerning this battle. If we have a relationship with Jesus Christ, we have victory! We don't need to be prisoners. And we can also be on the offensive in this war.

Check out King David's approach to battle:

I pursued my enemies and overtook them; I did not turn back until they were destroyed. I crushed them so that they could not rise; they fell beneath my feet (Psalm 18:37-38).

Question 1. Have you ever looked at lust as an enemy to overtake and totally destroy? Explain.

Nathan writes: "Much of my life from junior high through college, I lived as a victim of lust. I was always on the defensive, never the offensive. David's approach to battle was foreign to me. I never acted on my faith in Christ in a way that put me on the offensive; in fact, I never saw purity as a battle in the first place."

To continue in life-long purity, you must have an offensive strategy. This strategy must be built upon your strength, which is the person, Jesus Christ. Here are a couple of practical strategies to help you to be on the offensive in this war.

Offensive Strategy #1: View Victory!

The date is June 7, 1944:

Brigadier General Norman "Dutch" Cota, assistant division commander of the 29th, came upon a group of infantry pinned down by some Germans in a farmhouse. He asked the captain in command why his men were making no effort to take the building. "Sir, the Germans are in there shooting at us," the captain replied. "Well, I'll tell you what, Captain," said Cota, unbuckling two grenades from his jacket. "You and your men start shooting at them. I'll take a squad of men and you and your men watch carefully. I'll show you how to take a house with Germans in it." Cota led his squad around a hedge to get as close as possible to the house. Suddenly, he gave a whoop and raced forward, the squad following, yelling like wild men. As they tossed grenades into the windows, Cota and another man kicked in the front door, tossed a couple of grenades inside, waited for the explosions, then dashed into the house. The surviving Germans inside were streaming out the back door, running for their lives. Cota returned to the Captain. "You've seen how to take a house," said the general, still out of breath. "Do you understand? Do you know how to do it <u>now</u>?" "Yes, sir!"[24]

Question 2. What would "victory" look like for you?

Question 3. How can this story apply to battling lust and impurity?

In order to destroy the enemy of lust in your life you must act confidently on your faith in Christ, who gives us an example to follow in the battle, and has already won! Remember, apart from Him we have no strength, no victory. But connected to Christ, we are strong and victory is sure! "…in all these things we are more than conquerors through him who loved us" (Romans 8:37).

Years ago I (Nathan) played on a summer baseball team. This team was different than my spring high school baseball team. The main difference between the teams was that my summer team *expected* to win, whereas my high school team was *surprised* if they won. Guess which team won more games? The summer team did! We knew our strength, looked for the win and therefore played to our full potential! The battle starts in the heart, and in the mind! In this daily battle for purity, do you view victory through Jesus Christ and look for the win, or are you surprised if you win a daily battle? Remember the source of your victory, and you can view victory as you view Jesus Christ. Author and Pastor, John Piper says, "This is the most foundational strategy in the battle for joy – the strategic battle to see. By seeing the glory of Christ in the gospel, we are changed. In what way? Not first externally, but first internally."[25]

Do you know where your strength is? You have completed days 1-27. Hopefully, you've learned the power of an intimate relationship with Jesus Christ. Hopefully, you've radically amputated known sexual sin in your life. You're not yet perfect, but you've experienced some victory in this battle for purity. Remember, you're on the offense! Remember to be aggressive! Remember you're the <u>victor</u> instead of the victim through Christ who loves you! Do whatever it takes to live to your full potential in Christ. View victory!

Read these verses below and then answer the question.

No temptation has seized you except what is common to man. And God is faithful; he will not let you be tempted beyond what you can bear. But when you are tempted, he will also provide a way out <u>so that you can stand up under it</u> (1 Corinthians 10:13 emphasis added).

I can do everything <u>through Him</u> who gives me strength (Philippians 4:13 emphasis added).

Question 4. How are these verses important in helping you view victory and making you a victor, rather than a victim, in this battle for purity.

Offensive Strategy #2: Praise Jesus!

In this [future with Jesus Christ] you greatly rejoice, though now for a little while you may have had to suffer grief in all kinds of trials. These [trials] have come so that your faith, -which is of greater worth than gold which perishes even though refined by fire, may be proved genuine and <u>may result in praise, glory and honor when Jesus Christ is revealed</u> (1 Peter 1:6-8 emphasis added).

Question 5. What is God's ultimate desired result for the various trials and temptations you are facing?

    A. That you feel pain and know it's your fault

    B. That you lose heart and finally quit trying

    C. That your faith may result in praise to Jesus

Not long ago I (Jena) faced a battle similar to what we've been talking about. The battle was mainly in my mind and thoughts. After numerous failures at controlling my thoughts, I prayed that God would teach me how to win that battle. It was after that prayer, that I read the verses in 1 Peter 1:6-8 written above. I had the idea to start praising Jesus every time my thoughts started in a wrong direction. I decided that if Satan wanted to keep tempting me in my mind, he would have to put up with praises to Jesus every time. So, as goofy as it sounds, I promised that the next time my mind wandered toward sinful stuff, I would start praising Jesus, out loud, in as many ways as I could think of. Well, it happened the next morning in the car, my mind started wandering and I was reminded of my promise to praise. So there I was driving down the road, talking out loud about how wonderful and amazing Jesus is. (I'm sure people thought I was weird talking to myself in my car!) I was so focused on trying to think of bigger and better words to praise and thank Jesus that every other sinful thought left immediately! I didn't even realize how well it worked until I got home later that day. And that became my strategy from then on. Some days, I'd be talking and thanking Jesus before I even got into the car because the battle was so intense. But I was glad to know God was getting the results from me that He desired – praises to Jesus! And the evil one had to run away because that name of Jesus was so offensive to him!

You too can be on the offensive in this battle. Promise that you will take every thought captive and make it into praise toward Jesus, the Victor!

Question 6. What are some things you can praise Jesus for right now?

We demolish arguments and every pretension that sets itself up against the knowledge of God, and we take captive every thought to make it obedient to Christ (2 Corinthians 10:5).

Question 7. Please write your plan for taking every thought captive and making it obedient to Jesus Christ.

Remember, daily time with God is like spending time with your Commander and Chief. As you pray to Him and consult His Word (it's like a battle strategy manual) He will make clear to you places, people and things to avoid so that you can continue in life-long purity. Spending time with God fills your mind and heart with godly things that are powerful weapons and are offensive to the enemy. You will never lose when your heart is truly praising Jesus in an offensive, aggressive way. For when you are praising Jesus, you are focusing on and viewing the victory you desire! In Him is the victory!

Question 8. What were the two offensive battle strategies we talked about today?

1.

2.

Scripture to Consider

For the eyes of the LORD range throughout the earth to strengthen those whose hearts are fully committed to him (2 Chronicles 16:9a).

Did you live sexually pure today?
       Yes   *No*

Are you committed to staying sexually pure?
       Yes   *No*

Notes

DAY 29
Commitment to Purity

Today, we want to give you a place to make some commitments and share your testimony. It is important to solidify commitments and make goals now, as you are finishing this course, so that you can continually evaluate your pursuit of purity. Your own goals will be up to you. We will ask you to commit to a few things, but feel free to add to the commitment list according to your individual goals.

Will you commit to the following things, before God, yourself, and your accountability partner:

1. ❑ yes ❑ no   I will commit to pursue **purity** at all costs. I will be aware of the illusion from Satan that seeks to distract me and instead I will pursue God and what is **true**.

2. ❑ yes ❑ no   I will seek to daily learn and remember **who I am** in Christ.

3. ❑ yes ❑ no   Knowing the importance of purity before God, I will commit now and through the rest of my life, to **radically amputate** anything that causes me to sin.

4. ❑ yes ❑ no   I will commit to **radically consume the satisfying Living Water of Christ** through prayer and Bible study.

5. ❑ yes ❑ no   I will commit to **finding an accountability partner** this week, and maintaining complete honesty with them on a regular basis.

6. ❑ yes ❑ no   I will commit to **engage** in the daily battle for purity, and work to **implement the battle strategies** I have learned.

7. ❑ yes ❑ no   I will commit to **pray for and save my best for the mate** God has designed for me in the future.

8. ❑ yes ❑ no   I will commit to **becoming the kind of person** my future mate will need and desire in a God-blessed marriage.

Signature: _____   Date _____

Now here's the place for you to write your own testimony. Feel free to share however the Lord leads you, but keep in mind that the most effective testimonies are brief (usually 1 page in length), and should include **3 aspects**. Job 33 tells us the formula for sharing a testimony: *"Then he comes to men and says, I sinned, and perverted what was right, but I did not get what I deserved. He redeemed my soul from going down to the pit, and I will live to enjoy the light" (Job 33:27-28).* Notice the 3 aspects to this testimony: **"I sinned...God redeemed...I will live."**

A biblical testimony touches on:

> **My sin** and the areas in which I was involved, or **my wrong thinking** and what that brought about in my life (though be cautious about sharing any details so as to not stir up sin in others).
>
> **Redemption**. This explains how I was bought out of sin. How did God reach me, give me repentance and bring me into the Light? What has He taught me and used to show me reality?
>
> **How I am living now** to enjoy the reality of Jesus Christ and a life of purity?

Please try to include those 3 aspects in your testimony. Take your time. There are others in the same circumstances as you who will benefit from the lessons God has taught you. Writing down your testimony helps to solidify areas in your mind that you may not have clearly thought through. Please complete this step and feel free to look back (especially Days 1-3) and remember what the Lord has done for you. You may be able to use it and have an impact on someone you don't even know right now. Tell how God has altered your thinking and maybe include your methods for pursuing purity. May your story of God's grace honor the Lord.

Did you live sexually pure today?
　　　Yes 　　　　　*No*

Are you committed to staying sexually pure?
　　　Yes 　　　　　*No*

You may write your testimony here:

DAY 30
Passing On Purity

One day a little girl dressed in a white frock and carrying a great bunch of flowers passed a boy who was playing in the dusty street. Somehow the sight of that dainty figure stirred the spirit of mischief in the boy's heart, and he impulsively threw a handful of dirt, which struck the hem of the white dress and fell in a shower upon her shoes. The girl stood still. Her face flushed pink. Her lips trembled as if she would cry. But instead a smile broke over her face, and, taking a flower from her bunch, she tossed it to the boy, who stood waiting to see what she was going to do. No one ever saw a more surprised boy, or one more ashamed. He hung his head and his cheeks reddened under their tan and freckles. His unkind fun was quite spoiled, because in return for a handful of dirt someone had thrown him a flower. What a changed world this would be if everybody, big and little, were as wise as this six-year-old maiden![26]

This is a great story. Despite the little boy's actions, the girl threw him a flower. Instead of being overcome by the "dirt" thrown her way, she returned his action with a beautiful flower. She passed on something pure. Will you also pass on purity? Or do your actions in life throw dirt on others? This final day, we will talk about where to go from here in regard to your purity.

Yesterday you committed to eight things in regard to purity and you wrote your testimony about the changes you've seen God make in your life. Do you remember the eight item in your commitment of yesterday? This is key to being able to pass on purity.

Question 1. Please list the eight things to which you committed yesterday:

1.

2.

3.

4.

5.

6.

7.

8.

Today, the topic is passing on purity. That is an important part of making your own personal stand for purity real and galvanized. If you want purity, yet keep it hidden, apologize for it, and are ashamed of your stand, it probably won't be long until a more exciting illusion lures you into impurity. There is something powerful and authentic about sharing your conviction and influencing those around you by it.

What to Pass On

It is vital to know that you can't effectively pass on purity without passing on Jesus Christ. He is purity, therefore, He is the standard for purity. To attempt to influence others toward a lifestyle of purity without connecting them to Jesus is like influencing them to put out a fire with gasoline while you hold the water hose. Remember Jesus is the Living Water that satisfies and puts out the fires of impurity in our lives. Sharing that water with others is key to influencing them toward a life of purity. If a person does not know Jesus Christ as Savior, then the impurity in their lives is an outflow of the spiritual deadness from which they suffer. You must treat the disease in order for the symptoms to be altered. For non-Christians, their disease is their spiritual deadness. Only Jesus Christ can give a heart life and draw it toward purity. It is important for you to understand the core needs of those around you as you attempt to pass on purity.

Power of a Testimony

- "I worked out for 20 minutes 3 days a week and lost 100 pounds! Now I feel great about myself!"

- "I applied this cream twice a day and all my acne and scars are completely gone!"

- "This vegetable chopper has made my life so much easier! My family loves my cooking now!"

- "I have freedom and can go anywhere I want in this high-powered, attractive wheelchair. All my friends want one too!"

However real or far-fetched they may be, you've all seen the array of infomercials out there. Whether for health equipment, beauty products, cooking gadgets, or even wheelchairs, every infomercial centers around the testimonies of satisfied, happy customers. The companies are staking their business on the testimonies of these everyday people having an effect on us. Businesses don't underestimate the power of personal testimonies in their sales, and neither should we! Your testimony in regard to purity and your relationship with Jesus Christ is the most effective influencing tool you have! No one can argue with you about the real changes Jesus has made in your life. No one can discredit a life changed by Jesus. Your changed life is a powerful influencer! Don't underestimate it!

Your personal story of the battle and victories for purity in your life will ultimately open the door to give Jesus the credit he deserves. Remember, passing on purity means passing on Jesus.

Look at these personal testimonies of real people's interactions with Jesus, and note how they used their story to influence others around them:

The Samaritan woman: Read her encounter with Jesus:

When a Samaritan woman came to draw water, Jesus said to her, "Will you give me a drink?" The Samaritan woman said to him, "You are a Jew and I am a Samaritan woman. How can you ask me for a drink?" (For Jews do not associate with Samaritans.) Jesus answered her, "If you knew the gift of God and who it is that asks you for a drink, you would have asked him and he would have given you living water." "Sir," the woman said, "you have nothing to draw with and the well is deep. Where can you get this living water? Are you greater than our father Jacob, who gave us the well and drank from it himself, as did also his sons and his flocks and herds?" Jesus answered, "Everyone who drinks this water will be thirsty again, but whoever drinks the water I give him will never thirst. Indeed, the water I give him will become in him a spring of water welling up to eternal life." The woman said to him, "Sir, give me this water so that I won't get thirsty and have to keep coming here to draw water."

He told her, "Go, call your husband and come back." "I have no husband," she replied. Jesus said to her, "You are right when you say you have no husband. The fact is, you have had five husbands, and the man you now have is not your husband. What you have just said is quite true." "Sir," the woman said, "I can see that you are a prophet." Jesus declared, "Yet a time is coming and has now come when the true worshipers will worship the Father in spirit and truth, for they are the kind of worshipers the Father seeks. God is spirit, and his worshipers must worship in spirit and in truth." The woman said, "I know that Messiah (called Christ) is coming. When he comes, he will explain everything to us." Then Jesus declared, "I who speak to you am he" (John 4:7,9-19, 23-26 explanation added).

Now, see how this woman influenced others through her personal testimony of her encounter with Jesus:

Then, leaving her water jar, the woman went back to the town and said to the people, "Come, see a man who told me everything I ever did. Could this be the Christ?" They came out of the town and made their way toward him. Many of the Samaritans from that town believed in him because of the woman's testimony, "He told me everything I ever did" (John 4:28-30, 39).

Question 2. From the verses above, who did the woman tell about her encounter with Jesus?

Question 3. From the verses above, what was the response of the people after hearing this woman's testimony (verses 30, 39)?

In Acts 26, we can read how God's ambassador, Paul, understood the power of his testimony. As he stood before King Agrippa, with his life on the line, he resorted to his personal story. He told what he was, and he told what he had become. "I…was convinced that I ought to do all that was possible to oppose the name of Jesus of Nazareth. …I put many of the saints in prison. … I even went to foreign cities to persecute them." He went on to tell about how he encountered the living Christ on the road to Damascus and that he had traveled across the region and "preached that they should repent and turn to God. … I have had God's help to this very day. (Acts. 26:9-11, 20, 22) [27] Here was Paul's truthful story with which no one could argue!

So what is your story? Yesterday you wrote your testimony about how Jesus has influenced your life in regard to purity. Can you remember what you wrote yesterday? Is it still true today? Will you share your story and influence someone near you toward God and purity? Here is a testimony from a young man who has agreed to share what God has done in his life:

> **Josh, age 19, writes:** Before a friend directed me to Setting Captives Free, I was a borderline porn addict. I'd live free of it for a short time, then be tempted and once more would fall into it, each time getting worse. Over time, I began to see what this was doing to my life and relationships. I started to see it was killing me and I needed a way out. Jesus Christ was that way. It's not like I wasn't saved or anything. But there was a secret place in me I always kept from God, and it was filled with pornography, lust and various other sexual sins. Though I was still physically a virgin, I felt that I'd never be truly free from these secret sins.

However, the day I started this course I began to see what God's purpose in sexuality was and that it wasn't something dirty, but a gift to be given to that one special person you would marry one day. I started seeing where I'd believed all the lies Satan had once fed me, and since then, the feelings of emptiness have really subsided. I've seen that there is no temptation where God hasn't given us a way out. Though we may fall, if we come to Him and confess our sin he is very good to forgive us and help us to turn from it. Through the grace of God we all can be made free, and walk in that freedom as long as we put Jesus first! Now I live without all the guilt I lived with for so long, and have experienced God as I never have before! As Jesus said so long ago "Blessed are the pure of heart for they will see God". I am truly thankful not only for the friends that encouraged me to do this course but also for those who wrote it. Thank you so much!!

Question 4. Are you willing to share your story of Jesus' impact in your life - especially regarding purity - with another this week? Share your thoughts...

Yes   No

Be a Sweet Aroma

But thanks be to God, who always leads us in triumphal procession in Christ and through us spreads everywhere the fragrance of the knowledge of him. For we are to God the aroma of Christ among those who are being saved and those who are perishing. To the one we are the smell of death; to the other, the fragrance of life. And who is equal to such a task? (2 Corinthians 2:14-17).

Remember, purity in your life is not limited to just sexual activities. It is also tied to your conduct and your attitude in other areas. Living a pure life definitely means freedom from that which is not pleasing to God sexually, but it also means freedom from deceit, dishonor, and pride. Don't allow these qualities to be part of your life. Instead, be a sweet, pure aroma of Christ to others around you, rather than having an arrogant, "holier than thou" odor.

Question 5. In your own words, describe a "sweet aroma"?

Here are a few qualities of a "sweet aroma":

1. **A sweet aroma draws people.** Whenever I make cookies at home, my family can't stay out of the kitchen! They want to know where the good smell comes from and when they can have a bite!
2. **A sweet aroma invites others to experience it.** It is not enough to just smell a freshly baked chocolate chip cookie. Through its sweet aroma, you are invited to taste it and experience its warmth and goodness. When you are given a bouquet of roses or walk by a rose bush, it's not enough to see the flowers and just know they smell good, you are invited to experience it, to bury your nose in the petals and inhale the fresh fragrance they possess.
3. **A sweet aroma makes you want more.** Are you satisfied with only one freshly baked cookie? Chances are you find a way to sneak another one, or volunteer to eat the broken pieces. It is not enough to leave the beautiful smell of roses in the garden, instead, we surround ourselves with lotions, shampoos, room spray, body sprays, soaps that smell of roses, in order to give us more of the sweet aroma!
4. **A sweet aroma is not "it".** An aroma is just an outflow of what the object really is. The aroma leads us to the object. A smell of a baking cookie is not the ultimate. It is the object, the actual cookie that we enjoy! Why do we like rose-smelling lotion? It makes us think of the fresh beauty of roses out in the sunshine! The aroma is the air on the surface, and it always points to the true reality of what causes it. Your aroma, (your attitude, conduct) should not just be focused on a good "performance", but your aroma should point to the deeper reality, the deeper cause, of Christ in you.

A Leader Among Giants

To effectively pass on purity, we must remember the intense battle purity requires. Purity is not the easy road, nor is it the most popular. In fact, impurity acts more like a "giant" in our culture and our daily life. It doesn't seem able to be defeated by ordinary people, and it boasts of its strength and sure victory. Well, we can take courage from a young man in history that stood up to the challenge of the giant and won a great victory for God.

1 Samuel 17 describes the story of young David, the ordinary shepherd boy conquering the giant, boasting, warrior, Goliath. David's victory was a tribute to the powerful God he served. And God honored young David's courage by giving him a victory that is still noted over 2000 years later!

Read this story of David who was an amazing young leader against a real giant.